Cambridge Elements ≡

Elements in Research Methods for Developmental Science
edited by
Brett Laursen
Florida Atlantic University

LANGUAGE ASSESSMENTS FOR PRESCHOOL CHILDREN

Validity and Reliability of Two New Instruments Administered by Childcare Educators

Anders Højen
Aarhus University

Dorthe Bleses
Aarhus University

Philip S. Dale
University of New Mexico

CAMBRIDGE
UNIVERSITY PRESS

CAMBRIDGE
UNIVERSITY PRESS

University Printing House, Cambridge CB2 8BS, United Kingdom

One Liberty Plaza, 20th Floor, New York, NY 10006, USA

477 Williamstown Road, Port Melbourne, VIC 3207, Australia

314–321, 3rd Floor, Plot 3, Splendor Forum, Jasola District Centre,
New Delhi – 110025, India

103 Penang Road, #05–06/07, Visioncrest Commercial, Singapore 238467

Cambridge University Press is part of the University of Cambridge.

It furthers the University's mission by disseminating knowledge in the pursuit of
education, learning, and research at the highest international levels of excellence.

www.cambridge.org
Information on this title: www.cambridge.org/9781108927178
DOI: 10.1017/9781108924399

© Anders Højen, Dorthe Bleses, and Philip S. Dale 2022

First published 2022

A catalogue record for this publication is available from the British Library.

ISBN 978-1-108-92717-8 Paperback
ISSN 2632-9964 (online)
ISSN 2632-9956 (print)

Language Assessments for Preschool Children

Validity and Reliability of Two New Instruments Administered by Childcare Educators

Elements in Research Methods for Developmental Science

DOI: 10.1017/9781108924399
First published online: July 2022

Anders Højen
Aarhus University

Dorthe Bleses
Aarhus University

Philip S. Dale
University of New Mexico

Author for correspondence: Anders Højen, hojen@cc.au.dk

Abstract: This Element has two main purposes. First, it discusses purposes, advantages, and disadvantages as well as the challenges of different formats of language assessment, concluding with a focus on educator-administered language assessment in early childhood and education programs. It addresses the selection of assessment domains, the trade-off between brevity and precision, the challenge of assessing bilinguals, and accommodating the requirements of funders (e.g., government agencies) and users (e.g., educators and schools). It draws on lessons learned from developing two instruments for a national Danish-language and preliteracy assessment program. Second, it introduces those two educator-administered instruments – *Language Assessment 3–6 (LA 3–6)* and *Language Assessment 2-year-olds (LA 2)* – with respect to content, norming, gender, and socioeconomic influences as well as psychometric qualities. The intention is that this experience can help enable the extension of the educator-based approach to other languages and contexts while simultaneously acknowledging that linguistic and cultural adaptations are crucial.

Keywords: language assessment, preliteracy, vocabulary, school readiness, Early Childhood Education and Care (ECEC)

ISBNs: 9781108927178 (PB), 9781108924399 (OC)
ISSNs: 2632-9964 (online), 2632-9956 (print)

Contents

1 Introduction

1.1 The Danish National Early Language Assessment Project

This Element describes the development and psychometric properties of two language assessment instruments for Danish that were commissioned by the Danish government ministries for children and education. They were developed by the authors of this Element and their colleagues for use in early childhood education and care (ECEC) centers, to be administered by the children's usual ECEC educators. The background for this governmental commission was a heightened awareness of (1) the great variation in language development already apparent by the end of infancy (Fenson et al., 2007), (2) the association between early language development and later educational achievement (Bleses et al., 2016) and, further downstream, many other life outcomes, and (3) the realization that the provision of publicly subsidized early childhood care from about age 1 along with subsidized public ECEC centers, as well as free regular schools later, did little to close the achievement gap between advantaged and disadvantaged children.

The contextual factors that led to the development of these instruments are present in many other countries and regions, and the preparation of this Element was in part motivated by the belief that aspects of both the actual instrument and design and the process by which it was developed will be helpful to researchers and clinicians in other contexts. For closely related languages and similar cultures – for example, other Germanic languages and many other Indo-European languages with alphabetic orthography – a relatively straightforward adaptation might be made. For more diverse languages and writing systems, the process of reviewing basic language development research with an eye toward the practical evaluation of individual differences by educators, and evidence for its success, may be the most helpful contribution. In Section 5, we discuss some of the lessons learned from this project; some readers may find that section helpful before turning to the details of the specific Danish project.

1.2 The Purpose of Language and Language Assessment

The mastery of language is among the most central and significant accomplishments of early childhood due to its exceptionally wide range of functions that permeate individual and social life (Hoff, 2014; Luria, 1981; Wells, 2007). Language has a "public face" in its use for the communication of wants, information, emotional states, and relationships. It has a "private face" as well, as a tool for planning, thought, self-regulation and other aspects of executive functioning, and more. Drawing on both types of functioning, language can serve as a crucial tool for joint efforts and other forms of cooperation. The oral language skills developed in early childhood are also an essential foundation for literacy (Bleses et al., 2016; Harlaar et al., 2008), which will extend all the just-mentioned functions.

Consequently, variation in early language skills – impairments, variation within the normal range, and exceptional ability – has diverse and far-reaching consequences for almost all life domains, including education, vocation, social relationships, mental health, and life satisfaction. There has been an increasing worldwide awareness of and societal focus on this variability in recent decades. Several factors have led to the focus on variability. One is the overall contrast in success between oral language and literacy. The great majority of children (estimates of 93–95 percent: Leonard, 2014) growing up in environments free from the grossest kinds of deprivation attain oral language skills that, while variable, do not substantially impair participation in society. Fewer children – an estimated 80–90 percent – will attain levels of literacy that do not substantially reduce their life opportunities (Kamhi & Catts, 2012). Because literacy demands differ greatly across educational, occupational, and social contexts, there is no single criterion for success; literacy is best considered as a continuous variable for which low ability is an indicator of risk. However, variability in both early language skills and consequent literacy is substantially correlated with socially relevant factors such as poverty, low parental education, and immigrant status (Hart & Risley, 1995; Hoff, 2006). Thus it is connected to cultural values of opportunity and social mobility across generations. In addition, early language abilities do significantly predict literacy skills even beyond the prediction from the social factors mentioned here, a result that has motivated the examination of distinct aspects of early language development that may be particularly important for literacy. These issues are relevant and of social concern also in Denmark, a relatively affluent welfare society. In fact, social mobility in Denmark is relatively poor, particularly in light of the huge public investments in children and youth. Although Denmark ranks high on measures that are believed to facilitate social mobility, the often-cited Global Social Mobility Index is in fact a measure of presumed *drivers* of mobility, such as healthcare and education access (World Economic Forum, 2020). But income mobility in Denmark is largely due to redistributional policies, and educational mobility is comparable to that of the US in spite of Denmark's tuition-free education and monthly student benefits on which people can live while taking part in education (Landersø & Heckman, 2017).

The research findings just mentioned confirm that the rate of early language development can have a continuing influence, and consequently that effective early intervention has the potential to make a pivotal difference in a child's life. Early language development can either set an initial trajectory toward success and the fulfilment of potential or toward the risk of disappointment and failure. Of course, whether an assessment of delayed language development proves life-changing or not depends on the existence and accessibility of adequate follow-up procedures. In addition to the practical value for individual children, the systematic examination of large samples of language assessments is a powerful tool for researchers who seek to identify the range of factors and their interactions that influence children's language and early literacy development.

Thus, in the area of language development, as in most other aspects of behavior and development, assessment tools are central to valid work, both in research and in applied work such as clinical and educational practice. With respect to applied work, there are four broad functions of assessment (Snow & van Hemel, 2008). Each of them has its own set of features of highest priority; no one assessment instrument can be ideal for all of them. The first is *screening and prediction*; that is, identifying children who are at risk of later significant impairments. These children may or may not show current impairments (screening vs. prediction). For this function, the desirable properties of the assessment include rapidity of administration, minimal requirements for child compliance, and diagnostic validity, especially at the lower extremes of performance, not just correlations across the full range. The second is *identification of service eligibility*. Based on current performance, the results of longitudinal predictive research, and resource availability, some children can be offered interventions that go beyond the existing universal programs. Service delivery decisions are inherently based on a categorical classification, though it may be comprised of more than two categories, as in response-to-intervention (RTI) approaches (Fuchs et al., 2012). The criteria are somewhat arbitrary, because virtually all measures and predictive correlations are continuous, without all-or-nothing cut-off points. That is, in most cases we are dealing with quantitative variation along a dimension, not qualitatively different categories. For this function, the desirable properties of the assessment prioritize reliability and validity over cost, breadth of assessment (multiple aspects of language), and high-quality norms for the measure. The third function is to *obtain diagnostic information*, a more detailed characterization of the impairment that can guide the design of effective intervention for the individual child or group of children. For this function, the most desirable features of the assessment include sensitivity to the academic and cultural importance of the skills and an identification of good points of "leverage" for affecting the broader language system. Finally, the fourth function of assessment is to *evaluate the efficacy of the intervention*, which is a core concept of "evidence-based practice." Desirable properties of efficacy measures include repeatability for monitoring change over time, moderate cost in time and money, the inclusion of "near" and "far" skills relative to the intervention to gauge the generalizability of gains, and demonstrated sensitivity to change.

1.3 Typical and Atypical Development in the Preschool Years

The knowledge and skills that comprise competence in any language are complex and diverse. Linguists and others who study language often group them into four broad categories, all of which are developing in the preschool period (Hoff, 2014), although the exact number of categories and the boundaries between them vary across linguistic theories (e.g., Crystal, 2010). The first is *phonology*, the sound system of a language. Core aspects of phonology are the set of sounds used in the language and their contextually conditioned realization, along with the permitted sequential patterns of sounds; that is, the phonotactics of the language. For example, Bantu languages often include clicks – sounds produced by the intake of air (specifically, an ingressive, velaric airstream) – in contrast to the more frequently used sounds in most of the world's languages, which are produced by exhaling air from the lungs (specifically, an egressive, pulmonic airstream); Mandarin includes tones to contrast meaning; English has an unusually large set of vowels, and Danish an even larger one that, depending on the specific phonological analysis, outnumbers the set of consonants. The sequence *kn* is not permitted in English, though it is in certain related languages such as German or Danish; certain sequences of three consonants such as *str* are permitted in English but not in Japanese.

The second category is *lexicon* (alternative terms often used are vocabulary and semantics). It includes knowledge of the basic units of meaning, which are sometimes words and sometimes parts of words (derivational morphemes) that can be used to form new words by adding to a root word. For example, if *narg* is a verb, then a *narger* is someone who nargs. The prefix *un–* can be used to change the meaning of many adjectives into their opposite; for example, *unhappy, uncool*. Note that in a number of linguistic theories, knowledge with respect to units smaller than words is classified with morphology (and syntax) rather than lexicon.

The third category is *morphology and syntax* (sometimes collectively referred to as *grammar*), which is focused on combinations of the smaller units of meaning. It includes inflectional morphology, in which the addition of inflectional morphemes does not change the meaning of the word but adds something to it; for example, *dog* plus the ending *–s* means more than one dog. It also includes syntax – the rules for combining meaningful elements to generate a complex meaning. For example, in English, *The man bites the dog* means something different from *The dog bites the man* despite the identical words used; word order is a primary mechanism in this and many other languages. In numerous other languages, similar types of meaning difference are signified by the use of inflection and prepositions, while word order is more flexible, for example, in German or Spanish.

Finally, the fourth category is *pragmatics* – the knowledge that makes it possible to express one's own feelings and wishes, to comment, to make requests, and to perform other functions, as well as the ability to engage in coherent, meaningful conversation and narrative and to use context and knowledge of the world to help interpret intended meanings. Humor and irony are also important contributors to communicative effectiveness, as is the ability to indicate the speaker's view of the truth or validity of what is being said. For example, languages may have regular means for expressing the source of information and the speaker's confidence in it. An important component of pragmatics is the knowledge of how to be polite (or impolite, when that is the desired act).

Table 1 presents some major milestones of language development in these four domains between birth and school age (Hoff, 2014; Lightfoot et al., 2013; Saxton, 2017). It should be kept in mind that this information is based on the development of monolingual children in typical environments for their language community. The table is a broad summary generalization across languages, but it should be acknowledged that the largest body of evidence is on English and that there are variations across languages as well as language domains. In Danish, early vocabulary development is somewhat slower on average than for other European languages (Bleses et al., 2008b), and selected aspects of morphological development are slower than in other Nordic languages (Bleses, Basbøll, et al., 2011), whereas early phonological development, on the other hand, is relatively advanced in Danish children (Clausen & Fox-Boyer, 2017). However, at the level of detail reported here, the table is generally accurate.

It is also important to realize that these are just averages, and there is considerable variability even among typically developing children. There are moderate correlations among the various aspects of language development; there is also some evidence for causal effects among them, such as lexical development serving to stimulate morphological development, but it also appears that environments that are facilitative for one aspect of language are

Table 1 Some major milestones of language development in four domains during the preschool period

Phonology

Approximate age (months)	Milestone
Birth	Language universal phoneme perception Discrimination of language from nonlanguage sounds
6–7	Early babbling Beginning reduction of ability to discriminate non-native phonemes
10–12	Canonical babbling (CVCV sequences) with stress and intonation
30–36	Completion (or near-completion) of phonemic inventory
36–42	Beginnings of phonological awareness, e.g., rhyme

Lexicon

Approximate age (months)	Milestone
4–6	Recognizes own name
8–10	Understands a few words
12–14	Produces first word
18–20	50-word productive vocabulary Rapid growth in vocabulary ("word spurt")
28–30	500-word productive vocabulary
60	6,000-word vocabulary

Morphology and syntax

Approximate age (months)	Milestone
18–20	First word combinations
24–30	Grammatical morphemes (plural, past, etc.)
27–33	Negative and question forms
36–42	First complex (multiclause) sentences
42–48	Use of derivational morphology to understand and create new words

Table 1 (cont.)

Pragmatics

Approximate age (months)	Milestone
7–10	Use of vocalizations and gestures to attract adult attention, get desired objects and actions
14–20	Expanding range of communicative purposes of language, e.g., greetings, comments, requests for absent object
24–30	Increasing conversational initiative and responsiveness Correct response to indirect requests, e.g., "Is the door shut?"
30–36	Creation of indirect requests, e.g., "You're sitting on my dolly"
36–48	Development of narrative skills

usually beneficial for other aspects. In any case, the correlations are far from perfect, and that fact implies that in many situations, it is important to assess two or more of them. Also, given the near-universal use of vocabulary size as a measure, it is important to acknowledge that words differ in their ease of acquisition, even when the frequency with which they are heard by children is taken into account. For example, word class (nouns, verbs, adjectives, etc.), imageability of the word meaning (*dog* vs. *happy* vs. *idea*), and the number of similar-sounding verbs all influence the typical age at which particular words are acquired (Hansen, 2017).

The skills just described can be viewed as the primary oral language skills. All of them are foundational for literacy development, but lexicon and pragmatics are especially important both theoretically and for assessment. There is a large body of evidence that early vocabulary size is a predictor of later literacy (Bleses et al., 2016; Lee, 2011). One reason for the prediction is that for early readers, it is necessary to know a word in order to be able to read it; another is that the knowledge of other words in a sentence can facilitate the reading of each individual word and eventually learning the meaning of new words. Among pragmatic skills, the ability to understand and produce narratives is important for literacy (National Early Literacy Panel, 2008). Narratives – that is, stories – are the first step in mastering decontextualized language; that is, language about objects, people, and events remote in time and space. Ultimately, almost all print will be decontextualized in this sense.

There are other language skills, not as essential for face-to-face conversation but crucial for later literacy, namely preliteracy skills (Catts et al., 2015). For sound-based writing systems typical of European languages and many others, the most important of these, and among the best early predictors of literacy, are those that require awareness and manipulation of sounds (National Early Literacy Panel, 2008). For purposes of talking about a feline, *cat* can be considered a single unit; in contrast, to understand or generate rhymes – that is, to realize that some parts of the words *cat* and *hat* are the same and some are different – it is necessary to mentally divide the sound of the word into smaller units. This ability is an aspect of phonological awareness. A related test of phonological awareness is the deletion task; for example, "say window without dow" or "say sat without sss." Phonological memory – the ability to hold a sequence of sounds in memory and reproduce it later – is also highly relevant for literacy in sound-based writing systems. The nonword repetition task, which removes meaning as a possible cue in order to assess the purely phonological skill, is the most commonly used measure of this skill (Hoff et al., 2008). An example is "say volpitate."

There are other important pre-reading domains (National Early Literacy Panel, 2008). They include letter knowledge, both recognizing the shapes and having some sense of the sound they denote, and other concepts of print, such as the direction of reading a page (left to right vs. right to left), the order of pages, and an awareness of whether it is the pictures or the abstract shapes on the page – the letters – that are being read.

Although there is great commonality in language development within a language community, there is also great variation, particularly in rate of development, which motivates the development and use of assessments due to the predictive significance of early variation. The variation is seen even among typically developing children, as well as in children with specific impairments such as autism spectrum disorder, Down Syndrome, and Developmental Language Disorder (this clinical term is related to Specific Language Impairment but differs in that in Developmental Language Disorder, a nonverbal–verbal discrepancy is not required; the term is increasingly pre-ferred) (Paul et al., 2018). Most early impairments can be seen as delay in rate, rather than a qualitative difference. However, for certain clinical categories, there are also qualitative differences in the relationship among language com-ponents. For example, children with Down Syndrome often have relative strengths in pragmatics; children with autism spectrum disorder may not show the usual superiority of comprehension to production.

A wide range of biological and environmental factors influence or at least predict rate of development. Biological factors include genetic endowment, gender, and prenatal, perinatal, and other biomedical factors. Environmental factors include family socioeconomic status (SES; often indexed as parental education level), early language input (quantity and quality of child-directed language), and any intervention received. It is important to recognize that biological and environmental influences interact in multiple ways. For example, the input a child receives may be influenced by the child's gender, level of language ability, or simple talkativeness. SES may influence prenatal and perinatal experience due to, on the positive side, the availability of good medical care, and on the negative side, the influence of stress, poverty, or drugs. A family history of difficulty in learning oral language or reading probably presents both a biological and an environmental risk to the child.

Although many developmental disorders (e.g., Down Syndrome, Fragile X, autism spectrum disorder) have as one of their consequences impairment in language development, the majority of children with language delay do not present with such a primary disorder (Leonard, 2014). The language disorder *is* the primary disorder, though there may be some other closely related problems, such as with executive functioning or symbolic play. This fact is another motivation for the early assessment of language itself, as it may be the earliest sign of developmental difficulty. Nevertheless, it should be kept in mind that the significant overall prediction from early language delay to later development is still relatively modest (Dollaghan, 2013) and thus of limited clinical use by itself. Ideally it should be integrated with other types of information such as the nature of early language input, gender, and other factors listed previously (Rescorla & Dale, 2013).

An inherent challenge in all assessment of language is that while delay is a continuous variable, without any qualitatively defined "cut-off points" (Leonard, 2014; Rescorla & Dale, 2013), service eligibility generally requires a classification criterion. Although we have evidence that, overall, the more significant the delay early in development, the more likely it is that there will be difficulties later, that evidence still does not identify a specific criterion. Pragmatic issues such as the availability, nature, and cost of interventions are likely to determine the cut-off point to be used (but see the discussion of RTI in Section 1.4).

1.4 Language Assessment in an Educational Context

A broad characterization of the functions of assessment was presented in Section 1.2. In this section, which is focused on language and preliteracy assessment, we consider some of the most frequent purposes of assessment in an educational context (Snow & van Hemel, 2008). The most common of these is to identify children with specific individual needs relative to the goals and methods of the educational setting. Achieving this purpose may include screening if the assessment is just a first step, administered to all children, to be followed by in-depth assessment when indicated by the initial results, or it may be diagnostic, when the results are used directly in decisions concerning educational management and service delivery. An increasingly common variation on the diagnostic function is the core component of RTI approaches (Fuchs et al., 2012). Rather than applying a dichotomous classification criterion to all children, in RTI, continuous monitoring of children can lead to increasingly intensive interventions, first within the classroom and then moving to individualized services as needed. Conversely, good performance following that intervention will return children to the regular program. Language assessment may also serve to evaluate children's mastery of a second language, which is the language of instruction, to determine whether further second language instruction is needed. Low scores on these assessments need not imply that the student has an impairment, only that the level of mastery of the language of instruction in school is not yet sufficient for academic learning. Language assessment may also be a useful component of monitoring the effectiveness of interventions in many early childhood research projects when these interventions enroll children in the thousands, making research-based pre-testing and post-testing practically impossible. There is a growing awareness that the monitoring of effectiveness is important for everyday clinical practice as well; even educational programs using well-established curricula need to evaluate how well they are serving their students. Finally, language assessments provide a basis for providing feedback to parents, along with educator observations of their children's participation in the programs.

Informal observational assessment of language skills in an educational context has its own distinctive challenges. Both the group setting and the predominance of teacher-led activities imply that individual children have less opportunity to speak, and therefore there is less basis for observational assessment. Many contexts and topics of language use occur much less frequently, if at all, in the classroom compared to the home setting. On the other hand, new and important contexts will emerge or be more frequent in the classroom, such as language about more complex and/or abstract topics and responding to teacher "test questions."

Although both receptive and expressive language are essential skills and need to receive attention in assessment, receptive skills take on an even greater role in the classroom due to the emphasis in early education on introducing new concepts and relevant language for those concepts. This new language is much more likely to be mastered first at a receptive level rather than at an expressive level (Bornstein & Hendricks, 2012; Fenson et al., 2007). The effective assessment of receptive skills is often more difficult than noting whether the child can produce a word.

A third challenge reflects the increasing prevalence of bilingual and multilingual children with diverse other languages in the classroom (Hoff, 2015; Paradis et al., 2021). For these children, it is often the case that the language of instruction is a second language. Depending on the purpose of the assessment, it may be appropriate to assess only in the second language; for example, to evaluate the efficacy of instruction in second-language oral or written skills. But this narrow focus may be inappropriate when the goal is to decide whether the child has impaired language skills (Paul et al., 2018). For that purpose, assessment in the first language is also essential, but this prescription may be difficult when there are many first languages represented in the classroom, with varying availability (including none) of assessment tools in those languages (see Section 1.6 below). Note, however, that ambiguity in the interpretation of second-language assessment results is mainly confined to bilingual children who obtain low assessment scores. When bilingual children obtain second-language assessment scores within the typical range for native monolingual children, there is little reason to suspect impaired fundamental language skills.

Language assessment techniques for young children fall into three main categories (Marchman & Dale, 2018; Snow & van Hemel, 2008). The first is structured testing. Structured tests are highly efficient with respect to testing time, and they are well-suited for evaluating receptive skills; for example, with picture-pointing tasks. However, they do require a certain amount of time and, more importantly, training on the part of those doing the assessment, as both the administration and the scoring of individual items can be highly complex. Above all, they require the cooperation of the young child, which is particularly challenging below 2½–3 years.

A second assessment format is language sampling, widely used in basic research on early language development. A major strength of this observational technique is that it does not require the imposition of constraints on the child's behavior. However, it requires highly trained personnel for eliciting, transcribing, and analyzing the child's language. Transcription and analysis are extremely time-consuming. Two other limitations of language sampling are, first, that it is better suited for studies of language production than of comprehension and, second, that there are substantial contextual effects such that words and grammatical structures that are in fact within the child's repertoire may not occur in a given situation if the occasion does not arise. For example, words for extended kinship relationships (e.g., grandfather), toys, bathing, and sleeping are less likely to occur in the classroom, while more advanced words for spatial relationships, quantity, and time are more likely to occur there than at home.

A third approach has become increasingly common in studies of early child language, and that is parent report (Fenson et al., 2007). Parent report is based on extensive experience with the child, and experience that is highly diverse: at play, during meals, while bathing, at bedtime, and with themselves, the other parent, grandparents, siblings, and friends. The strength of parent report is that it represents an aggregation across a period of time and many situations, and thus it is less affected by contextual bias. Considerable research evidence has confirmed that parent report is most effective when it is focused on current function, not retrospective reports such as "When did your child say her first word?" and when it utilizes a recognition format rather than recall; for example, "Have you heard your child say green?" rather than "How many (or what) color words has your child said?" Although parents can often report on children's comprehension ability, this method appears most valid in the assessment of production. Recent research has extended parent report beyond vocabulary and grammar to other dimensions of language such as intelligibility (McLeod et al., 2015) and pragmatics (O'Neill, 2007).

1.5 Educator-Administered Language Assessment

Based on the generalizations that the most frequent purposes of assessment in early childhood education programs are screening and monitoring child language development and the effectiveness of ECEC intervention, that the nature of interaction in the classroom is distinctive in involving multiple children and linguistic predominance by educators, and that the resources available in terms of educator time and training are limited, educator-administered assessment in the form of reports and direct testing appears to be the most appropriate. Two such measures are the focus of this Element.

Parental report can also be of value, particularly with respect to the generalization of the linguistic skills that are the focus of the program to other settings and conversational partners. However, there are limitations to parent report as a primary measure of children in educational settings (Bleses, Jensen, et al., 2018; Dale, 1996).

Some parents may have low literacy levels, which hampers the validity of a questionnaire-based assessment (Roberts et al., 1999), and an interview format for the measure may be difficult or expensive to arrange. For some proportion of children of immigrant families, the language being assessed – the language of the classroom – is a second language, in which parents may have limited fluency and which they may not speak much at home. This linguistic mismatch is of even greater significance when some of the assessment is directed toward "pre-academic language" of numerical and spatial concepts, causality, classification, etc., which is less likely to be used in the home. In fact, a previous version of *LA 3–6* used parent report. However, feedback from educators gave the clear picture that obtaining these reports from parents was a huge and often frustrating task and that the reports were disproportionately often not completed by the parents of the children who, statistically, were at the greatest risk for language development issues, namely parents in at-risk families.

Educator-based assessment of language has several potential advantages as well as challenges. Educators have sustained experience with individual children, which is not available to more specialized professionals such as speech-language therapists, who may have only one session or a small number of sessions with a given child and who are, in any case, typically of limited availability in early childhood programs. At the same time, ECEC educators have experience with multiple children, providing a stronger basis for comparative evaluation among children than is possible for parents. They may or may not have received some training in language and/or assessment. They can provide both reports and simple test information about children. They are well-positioned to conduct repeated assessments to monitor the efficacy of intervention programs. There is also growing evidence that during the school years, teachers can provide valid assessments of, for example, reading (Dale, Harlaar, & Plomin, 2005). Another argument is that educators can use the result to improve language experiences for individual children as part of their educational practice.

Two recent educator-based language assessment projects have provided encouraging results. Both of the projects were based on adaptations of the MacArthur-Bates Communicative Development Inventories (CDIs; Fenson et al., 2007). Bleses, Jensen, et al. (2018) constructed a short version of the Danish adaptation of the CDI: Words & Sentences for 18–34-month-olds. The measure, *CDI: Educator*, included a seventy-item vocabulary checklist, for which words were selected from the longer *CDI: Words & Sentences* that were appropriate for educator classroom experience with children and also questions concerning the child's use of decontextualized language. The reliability and validity of the measure were judged adequate based on a sample of 5,097 children. Garmann et al. (2019) piloted the use of a Norwegian adaptation of the MacArthur-Bates CDI-III (Fenson et al., 2007), which is a brief measure for 3-year-olds. CDI-III reports from the parents of twenty-eight children were compared to those of educators in the children's ECEC centers.

The parents gave slightly higher scores than the educators did, but parent and educator scores were significantly correlated (intra-class correlations of between 0.47 and 0.71). In addition, CDI-III scores were correlated with spontaneous speech measures. CDI-III vocabulary scores were significantly correlated with number of word types in spontaneous speech (0.48), and CDI-III sentence complexity scores were significantly correlated with mean length of utterance in spontaneous speech (0.41). CDI-III grammar scores were, however, not significantly correlated with the number of grammatical errors in spontaneous speech. The authors concluded that educator reports of child language skills can provide good estimates of children's skills for some but not all language domains.

At the same time, there are challenges for educator-based assessment. Although the classroom (and the teacher's previous experience) provides a basis for comparison, it is inherently a divided attention situation, as the educator must attend both to other children and to the full range of goals of the program, including behavior management. Another challenge is the opportunity for bias, even if unintentional. The bias may stem from the belief that the program is successfully facilitating growth, or from expectations based on a child's previous assessment or other skills, such as social emotional skills. The potential challenge of bias applies to direct testing as well as to reporting; becoming an effective test administrator requires the development of skills to minimize unintentional cuing of the correct response or incorrect coding of responses that are not entirely clear (Sattler, 2001). Overall, testing requires a more skeptical perspective on a child's performance than the supportive perspective essential to good teaching, and this necessitates the careful wording of instructions.

1.6 Assessment of Children Learning Two or More Languages

The assessment instruments discussed in this Element are focused, with one exception to be discussed later, on the acquisition of Danish. Danish is the language of education in schools for virtually all children in Denmark and a key skill for successful experience in the larger society. Assessment of Danish is relevant and sufficient for determining how well children have currently mastered Danish, for identifying children who will need additional help, along with information for designing that help, and for evaluating ECEC programs. However, monolingual (here Danish-only) assessment is not sufficient or appropriate for determining whether a bilingual child has a language impairment in cases when bilingual children receive relatively low assessment results (whereas relatively high scores in the Danish assessment suggest no general language impairment, in which case Danish assessment is sufficient). This caution concerning low assessment scores is due to the fact that young bilingual children typically learn each of their languages at a slower rate than monolingual children learning that language (Bosch & Sebastián-Gallés, 2003; Hoff et al., 2012; Paradis et al., 2021). When competence in both languages is taken into account by adding measures such as vocabulary across languages, scores are quite similar for bilingual and monolingual children. These are not surprising facts; bilingual children have had less input in each language, because their experience is divided by language. And in fact there is much evidence that estimates by parents of the time spent in each language is a predictor of children's relative proficiency in each language (Hoff et al., 2012; Paradis et al., 2021).

The task of obtaining and integrating information about both languages in order to identify a language impairment is a very challenging one, given the increasing number of bilingual children and the number and diversity of other languages found in many countries, including Denmark, at present. For many languages there are no well-validated language measures, and even when they do exist, they are likely to require some ability in the language being tested.

Parent report measures are available for a wider range of languages, but they vary in degree of validation and in the extent to which some ability in the language is necessary to interpret the parent's responses. Educators cannot be expected to have the training and experience to deal with these issues or the technical issues of combining information from two or more languages. For this reason, there has been an attempt to develop a language-independent measure, one that could be translated into other languages as needed. Measures of this type typically consist of questions that rely on parents' general knowledge of children's language at this stage of life, such as "For your child's age, does your child have difficulty pronouncing words?" and "Do you have to repeat questions or directions to your child more often than to other children?" (Restrepo, 1998). As will be discussed in Section 3.5.4, a measure of this type is included in *LA 3–6*.

With some, albeit limited, information about mastery of the other language, along with information about the child's relative exposure to the two languages, it is possible to make an initial judgment as to whether there is an impairment. Nevertheless, when the evidence suggests a possible impairment is present, it is best to refer the child for more detailed evaluation by a speech and language professional who can call on more complex methods of assessment, such as dynamic assessment.

But why is it that establishing norms for bilingual language development is such a difficult, if not impossible, task? Bilingual or second-language acquisition varies depending on a range of developmental and contextual factors such as: At what age did second-language acquisition commence? How many languages is the child exposed to? What proportion of each language is the child exposed to? How closely related are the languages that the child is acquiring? Because of the multiple combinations of answers to such questions, a considerable number of disparate norms would have to be developed. To illustrate the difficulties, assuming four ages of learning the second language (ages 0, 1, 2, or 3), three levels of the amount of second-language input (approximately 25%, 50%, or 75%), there would be $4 \times 3 = 12$ basic contexts for children learning just two languages, with different developmental trajectories likely in each case. Separate norms would have to be developed for each minority language (e.g., Turkish, Arabic, Polish, etc.), meaning that to assess bilingual speakers of just the 10 largest minority languages in a given country fairly, 120 norms would have to be developed. However, even this calculation does not take into account children with more than two languages, and it also implies the very unlikely assumption that relative language input in the first and second language remains stable over time. Ideally, second-language norms should also be established for each language combination, doubling the size of the feat to be accomplished.

Even if time and money were no issue, it would be a practical impossibility to establish such norms, at least if the aim were norms with the same degree of quantitative robustness and age resolution (monthly) as those for the monolingual instruments described in Section 3.6. There are not enough children. In the light of these and other issues discussed in Section 1.5, our approach is to guide practitioners' interpretation of single-language (Danish) results for bilingual children by taking into account questions about the child's language acquisition history and context, such as those we have outlined. In addition, certain dimensions of language and preliteracy development are especially informative in the case of bilingual children, which will be discussed in Section 3.5.3.

2 Educational Language Assessment in the Context of a National Screening Program

Language assessment programs are typically placed in health services for reasons of accessibility, as is the case, for example, in Norway, which in many ways is very similar to Denmark, the focus of this Element (Klem et al., 2015). In contrast, the Danish language assessment instruments are designed to be administered by the educational staff in ECEC centers serving children aged 1 to 5 years and in Grade 0 (approximately age 6) as a tool to carry out the national language assessment program of children, which covers children in the age range of 2 to 6 years. According to current legislation (2020), each municipality must ensure that a language assessment is carried out for all children whom ECEC educators suspect may have nontypical or slow Danish language development and all children not in childcare. There are no requirements to use a specific language assessment instrument. However, regulations about who must have a language assessment have changed over the years.

In 2007, when the first version of the Danish assessment instrument was launched, the Danish government decided to implement language assessment for *all* 3-year-olds as an integrated part of educational practice in ECEC centers. Denmark has a near-universal ECEC system, and municipalities are obliged to ensure the availability of daycare for all families. Consequently, 97 percent of all 3–5-year-old children are enrolled in ECEC (Danish Ministry for Social Affairs, 2015). The number of infants and toddlers in ECEC has increased and, according to the Ministry for Children and Education, three out of four children are enrolled in ECEC even before they turn 3. On average, these children are about 10 months old when they start in center-based childcare or the parallel option of professionally supervised childcare in the private home of a home-based childcare provider (Ministry for Children and Social Affairs, 2018a). The universal ECEC system is therefore a highly suitable context for reaching nearly all children in Denmark.

By embedding the language assessment in an educational setting, the use of the Danish language assessment is broader than typical national assessment programs. The assessment instruments are intended to serve as a tool for the early detection of signs of language delays or disorders in individual children by assessing a broad array of language and preliteracy domains. However, at the same time, the instruments are intended to serve to inform the staff about the strengths and weaknesses of each individual child's Danish language and literacy development with the aim of tailoring the educational program to the needs of each child in the ECEC center.

The Danish government commissioned the researchers behind this Element to develop the instrument, taking into account the broader educational purpose of the language while at the same time ensuring scientific standards. Situational assessment in an educational setting has implications for the development of the instruments, in particular concerning the specific procedures used to assess each domain. For instance, even though nonword repetition is a standard procedure for assessing phonological awareness, we found via pilot testing that this task cannot be expected to be administered reliably by educational staff, who are not trained in phonetics. A consistent policy was followed in which otherwise plausible procedures or specific tests have been discarded because pilot tests demonstrated that educational staff could not administer them in a reliable way (e.g., the assessment of narrative skills).

A general lesson to be learned from embedding language assessment in an ECEC context with the purpose of assessing all or a great proportion of children is that educators may initially doubt whether they can do it. There may also be some initial resistance from some educators or factions within the ECEC community. However, our experience over the last fifteen years has been of a steady decline in resistance to language assessment in the ECEC context to the point where it is virtually nonexistant now.

3 A Language Assessment Instrument for 3–6-Year-Olds

3.1 Background

The first version of our language assessment instrument – *Screening instruments for 3-year-olds* (Bleses et al., 2010) – was developed on the basis of the available international research on the assessment of children's language development (see, for example, the report by Snow & van Hemel, 2008). The aim of this work was to identify the range of skills emerging in early childhood that have continuing predictive significance (including language development and early literacy) and to identify appropriate methods for measuring their development. Based on the view that the assessment of children (including language development) has one fundamental purpose, namely to support the best possible development of all children, the report recommends two general guidelines for the development of assessment materials: (1) the purpose of the assessment must be to provide a basis for decisions on the part of the ECEC center, and (2) the assessment should be part of a systematic and coherent effort that encompasses health, educational, and family aspects of the child's life. These two general guidelines have been followed in the development of the first and subsequent updated versions of the Danish-language assessment instruments described in this Element. It is also highlighted in the strong recommendation of the Snow & van Hemel (2008) report for the National Academy of Sciences that assessment materials must be evidence-based in terms of what is measured, how it is measured, and the way in which the measurement is subsequently used.

In keeping with these recommendations, the first version of the language assessment instrument from 2007, as well as all subsequent updates and new developments, was developed on the basis of a number of general principles: The selection of the language and literacy dimensions to be assessed is based on research documenting the relationship of early language and literacy skills to later reading skills. Subscales and individual items have been tested in multiple pilot studies. Standardized age- and gender-specific norms are provided. Fixed cut-off points for typical versus nontypical language development are established to standardize the interpretation of results. Standardized administration procedures have been developed and described. Internal and external psycho-metric properties are documented and are accessible to users.

Based on the requirements on the part of the Ministry for Children and Education and the research-based guidelines mentioned earlier in this section, the first version included subscales assessing language production (vocabulary, complex grammar, and pronunciation), language comprehension, and aspects of pragmatic skills (Bleses et al., 2010). As the name indicates, the first version targeted only 3-year-old children; that is, children around 36 months of age. The latest version, *Language Assessment 3–6* (hereafter *LA 3–6*), which is documented in this section, covers ages up to 6 years. Although the number and type of subscales have changed in several revisions in order to improve the reliability and validity of the instrument – using data from both norming studies and from "real-life" language assessments – the assessment instrument still assesses production, comprehension, and pragmatic skills.

Other revisions of the assessment have been implemented as a consequence of changes to the legislation governing the national language assessment program. In 2011, the age range of the language assessment instrument was expanded to include the assessment of children just before school start (age 5) (Bleses, Lum, et al., 2011). In 2015, the current language assessment instrument was finalized. The main change in the features compared to earlier versions is that the current instrument can be used to assess children in the entire age range from around 3 years (specifically 34 months) to around 6 years (specifically 71 months) with monthly norms, rather than being restricted to just 3-year-olds (version 1) or specific ages (version 2). Moreover, the language assessment instrument should make it possible to assess the development of Danish skills in children who acquire Danish as an additional language, but with detailed instructions provided in the manual on how to interpret results for this subgroup of children (see also Sections 3.5.3 and 4.6.3).

Given that the instrument measures several aspects of language and prelite-racy skills, it is important that each subtest is as compact as possible. Needless to say, a test session with lengthy subtests that drag on for an hour or more would not yield valid estimates of a young child's skills and, more importantly, would probably be an unpleasant experience for the child. In addition, in a context where ECEC educators administer language assessments to all – or at least a large proportion of all – children, expediency is important.

Therefore, via pilot tests, we have worked on reducing the number of items in each subtest to a minimum, which was still sufficient for obtaining a gradient in scores, although a normal distribution of scores was not always possible. One consequence of the move to limit the number of items is that we give age-dependent items for the subtests on Productive Vocabulary and Language

Comprehension. For these subtests, some of the items change between age 3 and age 4 and between age 4 and age 5. A downside of this approach is that raw scores are not comparable between ages. This, however, is not a real problem for use by practitioners because the raw scores are translated into percentile scores using age-specific (monthly) and gender-specific norms. The age-dependent shift in items is only a problem if researchers want to use raw scores. One solution to this problem is to apply the inverse normal distribution function to the percentile scores to obtain a normal distribution of scores that would lend themselves to typical statistical analyses. An alternative solution is to assume that older children who receive harder items know all of the easier items that were only administered to younger children. Each solution has advantages and disadvantages, but the design of the subscale was ultimately developed with priority given to making it a relatively quick and reliable assessment for use in an educational context, with research purposes having only secondary priority.

A reasonable question to ask is whether ECEC educators, who are not speech-language specialists, can reliably assess speech and language skills in children. In Section 3.7, we provide psychometric analyses that support the assumption that educators can do this. In addition, a recently published analysis of a precursor to *LA 3–6* indicates that measurement error is relatively low when ECEC educators carry out the assessment (Haghish et al., 2021). The version examined by Haghish and colleagues had a high degree of overlap with *LA 3–6*. The data used were pretest data collected for two parallel language interventions for 3–6-year-olds (Bleses, Højen, Dale, et al., 2018; Bleses, Højen, Justice, et al., 2018). Using hierarchical linear modeling (Raudenbush & Bryk, 2002) with the five levels – child, intervention group, educator, classroom, ECEC center – Haghish and colleagues were able to estimate the degree of measurement error associated with the educator level. The degree of estimated measurement error (or variance inflation factor) at the educator level ranged from 4 percent for the subscale Letter Identification to 19 percent for the subscale Rhyme Detection.

In the following sections, we describe the current version of the instrument *LA 3–6*. Note that the age range implied in "3–6" does not include ages all the way up to just before age 7 but rather from just before the 3rd birthday (34 months of age) until the last month before the 6th birthday (71 months of age).

3.2 Selection of Subscales

Based on international and Danish research on children's early language development (Bleses et al., 2007; Bornstein et al., 2004; Fenson et al., 2007;

Hoff, 2013, 2014; Wehberg et al., 2007), we identified important milestones in the language development of 3–5-year-old children (see Section 1.3).

The selection of individual items was based partially on previous research, as previously mentioned (Snow & van Hemel, 2008), and partially on empirical results from a large-scale study of 6,000 children aged 8–36 months (Bleses et al., 2008a) and 13,000 children aged 3–6 years (Bleses, Højen, Dale, et al., 2018; Bleses, Højen, Justice, et al., 2018) combined with educational expert knowledge and feedback from users.

We want to stress the importance of involving representatives of future users – that is, educators – in the development of the material. They may give information about limitations on facilities that may make an otherwise good test hard to administer in practice. In addition, information for users may help encourage the acceptance of the instruments. For example, many users may have an opinion on whether or not a given picture is a suitable picture to illustrate a particular word. Many users may believe that a prototypical illustration of a word, yielding high identification rates, is by definition the best illustration. This relates to the different goals of ECEC educators and speech-language therapists. Whereas speech-language therapists are trained to obtain accurate assessments of children, including exposing and identifying weaknesses, ECEC educators are trained to help children succeed.

Finally, as previously mentioned, it was critical for us to include only tasks and items that were practical and suitable for reliable use by educational staff who were not trained speech and language specialists.

3.3 Content

It was a requirement of the Ministry for Children and Education, which commissioned the instrument, that it be sensitive to language development across the entire scale of language skills; that is, ranging from children who are very delayed to the most advanced children. Thus this instrument contrasts with many other instruments whose primary purpose is to identify children with poor language development and therefore do not distinguish between children with typical versus advanced language development. If, however, equivalent sensitivity across the entire range of skills could not be obtained, sensitivity at the low end of scores was a priority for our instrument.

In order to ensure that developmentally appropriate items are administered to children at each age within the target range, the items used at the three ages change somewhat in the Vocabulary and Language Comprehension subscales, as noted. For the Vocabulary subscale (twenty-five items), ten items were changed between ages 3 and 4 and between ages 4 and 5. In other words, the overlap between ages 3 and 4 and between ages 4 and 5 comprised 60 percent of the items. The overlap between age 3 and age 5 was 20 percent. For the Language Comprehension subscale (twenty items), five items changed between age 3 and age 4 and between age 4 and age 5. In other words, the overlap between ages 3 and 4 and between ages 4 and 5 comprised 75 percent of the items. The overlap between ages 3 and 5 comprised five items or 50 percent.

The instrument consists of subscales measuring oral language skills as well as subscales measuring preliteracy skills. Table 2 provides an overview of the subscales and the ages at which they are administered. Note two distinct types of age dependency in the administration: (1) whether or not a subscale is adminis-tered at a given age, and (2) whether the particular items administered are age dependent.

3.4 Administration

For the administration of *LA 3–6*, the following materials have been developed (see Table 3). All materials have been developed for paper format but have been integrated into an IT platform by commercial as well as governmental suppliers, the latter offering the platform free of charge. The purpose of IT platforms is to facilitate the easy and consistent implementation of the measure, along with the recording of responses and the conversion to norm-based percentile scores for documentation of the individual child's skills and skill development over time. The platform enables educators to use a tablet or laptop computer to read directions and record the child's responses. Some platforms also enable the visual presentation of stimuli, although to optimize comparability with the presentation mode of stimuli in the norming study, we recommend presenting

Table 2 Subscales of *LA 3–6*

	Subscale	Test type	Items per age	Age of administration
Language	Vocabulary[1]	Test	25	3–5
	Comprehension[1]	Test	20	3–5
	Communicative Strategies	Checklist	15	3–5
Preliteracy	Rhyme	Test	15	3–5
	Print Awareness	Test	16	4–5
	Letter Naming	Test	12	5
	Deletion	Test	15	5

[1] Items are age dependent

Table 3 Overview of which materials are used for which parts of the assessment process

Material	Administration	Results	Interpretation	Intervention
Assessment form	✓			
Picture booklet	✓			
Results report (IT system)		✓	✓	✓
Supplementary questions to parents			✓	
Manual	✓	✓	✓	

stimuli from a picture booklet. That said, it is an open question whether contemporary and future children who may be more familiar with tablets than with books are comparable in this regard with the children in the norming study, which was conducted in 2015, when young children were probably less familiar with tablets.

3.4.1 Assessment Form

The assessment form includes all subscales (i.e., Vocabulary, Rhyme Detection, etc.) and their associated test items. For each subscale there is a brief guide containing a description of the subscale, information about which materials are to be used, and a description of how to perform the assessment task with the child (e.g., rhyming task or language comprehension task) and how it is scored. The child's response can be manually recorded on paper and subsequently entered in the IT system, or it can be registered directly in the IT system. This requires that the assessor has a computer or tablet at hand; feedback from users indicates that some experience is required to use a computer or tablet for registering the child's response while at the same time keeping a full focus on the child in order to keep the child engaged in the tasks.

3.4.2 Assessment of the Child on Each Subscale

Four of the assessment subscales require the use of materials for the child to look at; that is, pictures or letters. These subscales are Language Comprehension, Productive Vocabulary, Rhyme Detection, and Letter Knowledge. Examples of these are shown in Figures 1–3.

For Language Comprehension, the child is asked to choose one of four pictures corresponding to a sentence uttered by the administrator; for example: *Where is the boy being chased by the dog?* (see Figure 1).

Figure 1 Example of pictures for Language Comprehension. The child has to point to one of four pictures corresponding to a sentence uttered by the administrator

Figure 2 Example of word elicitation pictures for Productive Vocabulary assessment. Contrasting pictures are used to elicit less tangible or illustratable words such as "drinking": *The woman is eating. What is the man doing?*

For Productive Vocabulary, the child is asked to label an element of a picture. Two-thirds of the words are nouns, two words are adverbs (place and time), and the remaining words are approximately equal numbers of adjectives and verbs. For nouns, the child is simply asked *What is this?* For other categories, where it might not be obvious which of the multiple elements of the picture is to be

Figure 3 Example of pictures for a Rhyme Detection item using the three words *hus* [huːˀs] ("house"), *mus* [muːˀs] ("mouse"), and *sol* [soːˀl] ("sun").

named, two contrasting pictures are given to help elicit the relevant word; for example: *The woman is eating. What is the man doing?* (see Figure 2).

For Rhyme Detection, three pictures are shown, and the child is asked to point to the two pictures of objects whose names are words that rhyme. The administrator names the three pictures and asks the child to point to "the two things that sound alike; those that rhyme" (see Figure 3).

For assessment of Letter Knowledge, twelve capital letters are shown in a table, and the child is asked to name each of the letters: I C J F E G O S A L D K. There are twenty-nine letters in the Danish alphabet. Testing all letters would be time consuming, and therefore a subset of letters was identified and used in a previous version of the instrument and carried over to the present version.

The Deletion task has three blocked levels of difficulty that require the child to say what is left when deleting (1) one word-part of a compound (e.g., *Say snowman without man*), (2) deleting a syllable, (e.g., *Say window without dow*), or (3) deleting a sound (e.g., *Say cold without khh*). The deleted part could be either at the beginning or the end of the word. The remaining part of the word would always make a word in its own right (such as *snow*, *win*, and *old* in the English examples).

For the assessment of Print Awareness, the assessor uses a picture book of their own choice (not provided with the test). The book must have both text and pictures. The assessor asks the children sixteen questions related to book reading, generally increasing in difficulty, starting with handing the book to the child and asking *What is this?* Later questions pertain to where to start reading on a page and pointing out examples of a word, the last word on a page, or the last letter in a given word.

For assessment of the child's communicative skills, the child is not directly involved. An educator who is familiar with the child from day-to-day care rates how frequently (never, seldom, often, or always) a child would give a particular communicative response in a hypothetical communicative situation. For example, *A child or an adult talks to the child on the playground. The child reacts by answering the other child/the adult.* More advanced examples include *You are talking to the child, but the child seems to not understand. The child asks clarifying questions* and *At home, the child has heard their parents talk about an experience. The child explains to you what the parents were talking about.*

3.5 Results of the Assessment

3.5.1 The Results Report

Based on the number of items responded to correctly and the age and gender of the child, the child's performance can be compared with norms (available to potential IT platform contractors upon request from the Danish Ministry of Education). The resulting report contains two overall summary scores in terms of percentiles: a language summary score and a preliteracy summary score. The language summary score is generated by standardizing the language subscale scores (Vocabulary, Language Comprehension, and Communication), averaging the scores, and subsequently converting them to percentile scores (see Section 3.7.4). Likewise, the preliteracy subscale scores (Rhyme, Print Awareness, Letter Naming, and Deletion) were standardized and averaged to generate the preliteracy summary score. Note, however, that the administration of preliteracy subscales depends on age (see Table 2). Because the only subscale administered to 3-year-olds is Rhyme, no preliteracy summary score is generated for 3-year-olds. The mean score for each of the summary scores is referenced against the norms for the child's age and gender to produce a language summary percentile score and a preliteracy summary percentile score.

The report also shows the percentile scores of each of the subscales completed by the child to help generate a "language profile" for each child; that is, a profile showing which dimensions of language or preliteracy skills are strong or weak in the child. The two summary scores and the language profile scores also indicate the age- and gender-specific 5th and 15th percentiles. An example of a results report is given in Figure 4 for a fictional child.

The 5th and 15th percentile cut-off points were set to facilitate the best use of later resources. The requirements of later intervention based on the results of individual children were operationalized into three levels of skill development for each subscale as well as for the summary scores for language and preliteracy – (1) "low" (percentiles 1–5), (2) "at-risk" (percentiles 6–15), and (3) "typical" (percentiles 16–100) – for determining the language support and educational needs of each child. Rather than outputting the categories low, at-risk, and typical for each child, the report assigns a corresponding intervention category; namely, "Special intervention" (percentiles 1–5), "Focused intervention" (percentiles 6–15), and "General intervention" (percentiles 16–100).

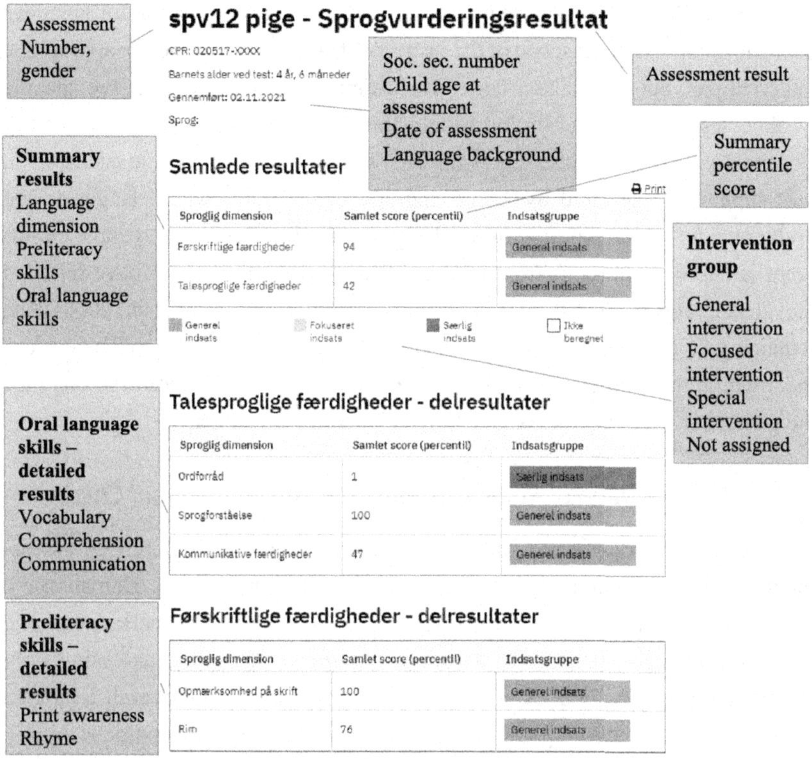

Figure 4 Example results report showing percentile scores
for the two summary scores and some of the individual subscale scores for
a fictional child

Although using percentiles has the advantage of yielding comparable scores across ages, we have also consistently found that the concept of percentiles is difficult to communicate to users who are ECEC professionals but not necessarily used to manipulating numbers. However, it is usually possible to explain the concept by beginning with the concept of halves, the upper half and the lower half of scores, then progressing to the concepts of quartiles, deciles, and percentiles.

3.5.2 Interpretation of Results

We recommend in the manual that the lowest-scoring 5 percent of the children should be referred to a professional speech therapist in order to conduct a complete professional pathological speech assessment and potentially to receive specialized intervention. This cut-off point corresponds to the existing mean referral rate to speech therapists across municipalities in Denmark for 3-year-olds at 4.3 percent (Reusch, 2006). Children with scores between 6th and 15th percentile are referred to the ECEC center for focused intervention and a later reevaluation for language delay. It is not within the scope of the instrument and manual to specify appropriate interventions, but the manual does give examples of how to target the specific weaknesses of a child according to their profile (e.g., low scores on Rhyme or Vocabulary). The percentile scores for each subscale may help guide educators in best supporting the child by identifying specific domains within language and preliteracy for which the child needs the most support. The 15th percentile cut-off point is based on findings from studies of language delay, which have reported prevalence rates ranging from 2.3 percent to 19 percent (Nelson et al., 2006). The remaining 85 percent of the children can be regarded as having language development within the normal range. Thus these children are recommended to continue the general or usual instructional activities in the ECEC center.

3.5.3 Interpretation of Results for Bilingual and Multilingual Children

The *LA 3–6* was developed specifically to provide a norm-referenced assessment of Danish language development in children learning Danish only. However, a large and growing proportion of children in Denmark speak one or more languages at home in addition to Danish. Therefore, assessing only Danish-language skills does not provide a full picture of the overall language skills of children learning multiple languages. Although it would be highly useful to establish norms for bilingual children – either for both/all of a child's languages or just the majority language – this is not feasible, because no one set of norms would be sufficient, as discussed in Section 1.6.

With the given limitations of only assessing the majority language – Danish – in bilingual and multilingual children, it is important to give extra attention to the interpretation of their assessment results, as their development is highly variable. First, even though more bilingual than monolingual children score below the 15th percentile cut-off point, a large number of bilingual children do not. For these children, there is little reason to suppose that they have any problems with language development, because they score within the typical language development range for monolingual children even in their second language. Second, educators are advised to base their evaluation of the child's language development more on preliteracy subscales than on oral language subscales. This is because bilingual children have been found to resemble or even exceed monolingual children with respect to preliteracy skills such as rhyming, deletion, and letter knowledge, presumably because such skills translate better between languages than do oral language skills and/or because the bilingual experience facilitates better metalinguistic and phonological awareness (Hammer et al., 2014; Højen et al., 2019; Højen et al., 2021). Therefore, low scores on, for example, Vocabulary and

Language Comprehension should raise less concern if the child scores highly on, for example, Rhyme and Deletion than if the child generally scores low on both oral language and preliteracy subscales. In the former case, it is likely that the child has had too little exposure to Danish to score within the typical range for oral language skills. Educators are encouraged to seek information from the child's parents about when the child began to be regularly exposed to Danish and the proportion of Danish input in order to best interpret low scores in the language assessment.

3.5.4 Supplementary Questions for Parents of Bilingual and Multilingual Children

To provide additional help with the interpretation of the assessment results of these children, we compiled ten language-independent questions in a questionnaire inspired by Restrepo (1998). The questions are primarily for parents of bilingual children with low percentile scores in the language assessment. In these cases, it is crucial, but difficult, to determine whether the low scores are due to general language learning difficulties or due to the child being in the early phase of Danish second-language acquisition. The questions for parents are given in Table 4.

As the wording shows, the questions must be answered with reference to the child's age, and as such, the questions require some insight from the parents with respect to normal language development. The questionnaire was developed as an addendum to *LA 3–6* and has not been validated. Therefore, it should be seen as a tool to help interpret the results of bilingual children when they receive low scores in the *LA 3–6* proper, along with any other information available on the child's mastery of the first language. The questions may be answered for just the minority language spoken at home or for both the minority and the majority language.

3.6 Norming Study

A norming study was conducted to develop age-specific (monthly) and gender-specific norms based on a population-representative sample of children. The norms were expressed as percentile scores, so that in later use of the instrument, it could be determined that a raw score of, for example, 14.5 on a subscale for a 40-month-old girl corresponds to a percentile score of 55; that is, a little above the median. For a 44-month-old girl, the same raw score would correspond to a slightly lower percentile score; for example, 45. One advantage of percentiles over standard scores is that percentiles are more accurate in identifying low extreme levels.

Table 4 Supplementary questions primarily for parents of bilingual children to help educators determine whether low scores on the Danish majority language assessment are indicative of general language learning difficulties or due to the child being in the early phase of majority language acquisition

Language domain	Specific question
General	1. For your child's age, does your child have problems communicating with you?
	2. Do your friends or family think that your child is delayed in talking?
	3. Did either of the parents have difficulties learning to talk or learning to read?
Pronunciation	4. For your child's age, does your child have difficulty pronouncing words?
	5. Do your friends or family think that your child is difficult to understand?
Vocabulary	6. Do you think your child has difficulty learning new words?
	7. Does your child often point or use a general word like "that thing" rather than the specific word; for example, "the ball"?
Grammar/ production	8. For your child's age, does your child produce very short sentences?
	9. Is it hard to tell if your child is talking about one or more objects or people, because your child uses the words incorrectly? For example, saying "I got a good friends."
	10. For your child's age, do they often make mistakes when talking about things in the past? For example, saying "Yesterday, I play with Tom!"

3.6.1 Sample

The norming study of the *LA 3–6* used baseline (pretest) data from a two-year randomized controlled trial study of the effectiveness of an intervention (The Daycare of the Future, Nielsen et al., 2017) targeting language, cognitive skills, and social emotional skills in children aged 0–6 years, funded by the Danish Ministry for Children and Social Affairs. Fourteen municipalities participated. They were selected from a pool of interested municipalities to represent geographically disparate parts of Denmark as well as urban profiles and rural profiles and were thus representative of Danish municipalities. A total of 442 home-based care units and 145 ECEC centers were included, encompassing a total of 10,948 children aged between 0 and 6 years, but only children in the age range 34–71 months who had Danish as their first language were included in the norming study of *LA 3–6*. The *LA 3–6* was administered to children in the included ECEC centers by educational staff over a six-week period in August/ September 2014 using the professional online documentation system Rambøll Results. The educational staff had already administered the prior version of the language assessment instrument as part of the national language program but received local introductions to the changes introduced in *LA 3–6*.

The sample was representative with respect to age, gender, and the distribution of maternal educational background. The mean years of formal education for the mothers of the 3–5-year-olds in the sample was 14.6 years (SD = 2.8) for the year 2014, which was virtually the same as for the general population of mothers (14.6 years, SD = 2.5), though just for mothers of 4–5-year-olds and for the year 2012. Table 5 gives more detailed information about the sample.

An important note is that, as is often the problem with large-sample research conducted in the broader population, there is missing data for both background measures and outcome measures. Therefore, in the description of subscale scores in the following sections, the *N* for each subscale is given.

3.6.2 Descriptive Statistics for All Subscales

Descriptive statistics for the summary scores of the subscales of *LA 3–6* for each age group are shown in Tables 5–18 and Figures 5–11. For data protection reasons, minimum and maximum values have been obscured if certain scores

Table 5 Descriptive statistics of the norming sample by age, gender, and maternal education

	Variable	*N*
Age	3 years	3,822
	4 years	3,914
	5 years	3,212
Gender	Boys	5,634
	Girls	5,282
	Missing gender info.	32
Maternal education	Short (basic schooling)	1,485
	Short-mid	4,227
	Mid-long	3,437
	Long (BA or higher)	1,460
	Missing education info.	339

have been obtained by fewer than three individuals. Likewise, histogram bins most often encompass several scores in order not to show scores obtained by fewer than three individuals. To examine the robustness of the results, we randomly divided the recruited children into two groups for each age group, and we report the split sample results. Skewness (degree of asymmetry of the distributions) and kurtosis (degree of outliers/heavy-tailed distribution) are indicated for both whole and split samples and statistically tested for whole samples.

Table 6 and Figure 5 present descriptive statistics and histograms for the Vocabulary subscale. Because there is a change of items across ages for this subscale (Section 3.3), the scores are not directly comparable across the age groups. The histograms are more informative, as they demonstrate that variability in this skill is appropriately captured, the degree of skewness is visualized, and any floor or ceiling effects are detected. Although there is a modest degree of skew – significant right skew for age group 3, significant left skew for age groups 4 and 5 – neither floor nor ceiling effects are apparent.

Table 7 and Figure 6 present descriptive statistics and histograms for the Language Comprehension subscale. Like Vocabulary, the Language Comprehension items change somewhat between ages, and consequently the mean levels cannot be compared. The Language Comprehension histograms show a somewhat higher degree of skewness than for Vocabulary, all left-skewed, and a modest ceiling effect that is comparable across the age groups. The left-skewed distribution is in line with our intention, along with obtaining valid measures across the full range of performance, to obtain special sensitivity at the low end of the scale – or in other words, "err on the side of left-skewness" – if a normal distribution could not be obtained.

Table 8 and Figure 7 present descriptive statistics and histograms for the Communication subscale. For this subscale, the items do not change with age, and thus the means in Table 7 and the relative "peaks" in Figure 7 demonstrate the degree of change with age. At ages 3 and 4, there is only a modest degree of skewness and little evidence for a ceiling effect. However, at age 5 there is a strong ceiling effect and a corresponding high degree of left-skewness, which need to be taken into account when interpreting scores on this subscale at that age. But again, our priority is sensitivity to skill differences at the low end of scores.

Table 9 and Figure 8 present descriptive statistics and histograms for the Rhyme subscale. As the items on this subscale do not change with age, the means demonstrate growth in this ability. As rhyme detection is known to reach mastery level in the preschool years in literate societies, there is an

Table 6 Mean scores, standard deviations, range, and distributional characteristics for the subscale Vocabulary for 3-, 4-, and 5-year-olds. Values for the two split sample groups are Age-dependent items.

Vocabulary	N	Missings	Mean	SD	Range	Skewness	Kurtosis
3-year-olds	3,624	198	11.1	5.3	0–25	0.10[1]	2.34[1]
Split sample	1,809/1,815		11.3/10.9	5.5/5.2	0.25/0.25	0.04/0.15	2.29/2.38
4-year-olds	3,790	124	14.0	4.8	0–25	−0.29[1]	2.66[1]
Split sample	1,890/1,900		14.0/14.0	4.8/4.7	0.25/0.25	−0.25/−0.33	2.65/2.67
5-year-olds	3,139	73	14.7	4.3	0–25	−0.41[1]	2.93
Split sample	1,576/1,563		14.5/14.8	4.3/4.3	1–25/0–25	−0.35/−0.46	2.80/3.07

[1] Skewness/kurtosis test for normality significant, $p < 0.05$.

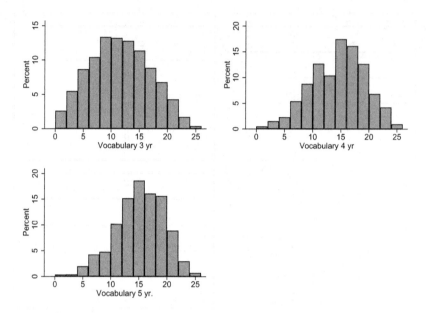

Figure 5 Distribution of scores on the Vocabulary subscale for children aged 3, 4, and 5 years. Age-dependent items

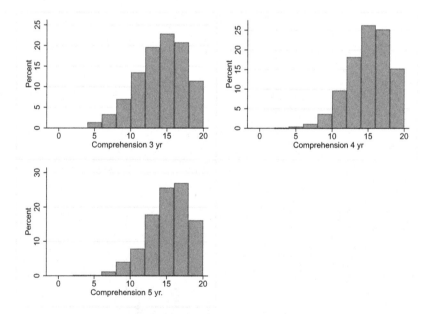

Figure 6 Distribution of scores on the comprehension subscale for children aged 3, 4, and 5 years. Age-dependent items

Table 7 Mean scores, standard deviations, range, and distributional characteristics for the subscale Language Comprehension for 3-, 4-, and 5-year-olds. Age-dependent items. Values for the two split sample groups

Comprehension	N	Missings	Mean	SD	Range	Skewness	Kurtosis
3-year-olds	3,734	88	13.6	3.3	<4–20	−0.51[1]	2.94
Split sample	1,871/1,863		13.6/13.6	3.4/3.3	<4–20/<4–20	−0.49/−0.53	2.85/3.02
4-year-olds	3,884	30	14.5	2.9	<4–20	−0.55[1]	3.27[1]
Split sample	1,941/1,943		14.5/14.6	2.9/2.8	<4–20/<5–20	−0.56/−0.54	3.27/3.26
5-year-olds	3,186	26	14.7	2.9	3–20	−0.58[1]	3.16
Split sample	1,595/1,591		14.7/14.7	2.9/2.9	5–20/3–20	−0.50/−0.66	2.94/3.38

Note: For data protection, minimum and maximum scores are given using operators (<) if at least one score below or above the reported minimum/maximum is obtained by fewer than three individuals.
[1]Skewness/kurtosis test for normality significant, $p < 0.05$.

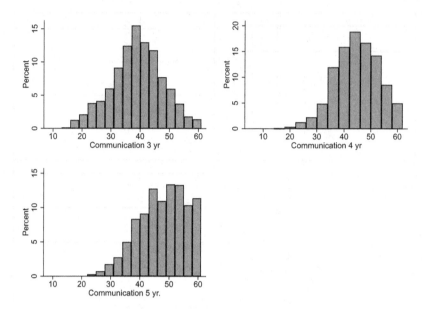

Figure 7 Distribution of scores on the Communication subscale for children aged 3, 4, and 5 years

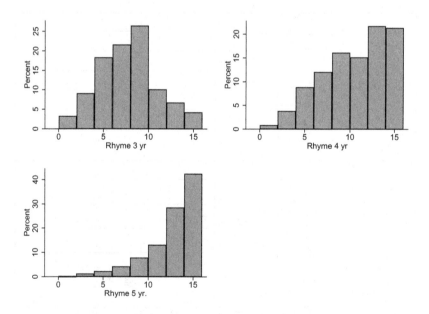

Figure 8 Distribution of scores on the Rhyme subscale for children aged 3, 4, and 5 years

Table 8 Mean scores, standard deviations, range, and distributional characteristics for the subscale Communication Skills for 3-, 4-, and 5-year-olds. Values for the two split sample groups

Communication	N	Missings	Mean	SD	Range	Skewness	Kurtosis
3-year-olds	2,774	1,048	38.4	8.8	15–60	−0.13[1]	2.82[1]
Split sample	1,382/1,392		39.0/38.0	8.8/8.7	15–60/15–60	−0.11/−0.15	2.83/2.80
4-year-olds	2,686	1,228	44.2	8.2	<19–60	−0.24[1]	2.77[1]
Split sample	1,329/1,357		44.3/44.2	8.2/8.1	19–60/<19–60	−0.26/−0.22	2.78/2.75
5-year-olds	2,127	1,085	47.2	8.3	15–60	−0.49[1]	2.83
Split sample	1,045/1,082		47.2/47.2	8.4/8.2	15–60/15–60	−0.57/−0.40	3.05/2.59

Note: For data protection, minimum and maximum scores are given using operators ($<$) if at least one score below or above the reported minimum/maximum is obtained by fewer than three individuals.

[1] Skewness/kurtosis test for normality significant, $p < 0.05$.

Table 9 Mean scores, standard deviations, range, and distributional characteristics for the subscale Rhyme for 3-, 4-, and 5-year-olds. Values for the two split sample groups

Rhyme	N	Missings	Mean	SD	Range	Skewness	Kurtosis
3-year-olds	2,730	1,092	7.3	3.2	0–15	0.18[1]	2.68[1]
Split sample	1,384/1,346		7.1/7.4	3.2/3.3	0–15/0–15	0.12/0.22	2.73/2.63
4-year-olds	3,593	321	10.1	3.6	0–15	−0.49[1]	2.27[1]
Split sample	1,789/1,804		10.1/10.1	3.6/3.6	0–15/0–15	−0.53/−0,46	2.33/2.22
5-year-olds	3,065	147	12.2	2.8	<3–15	−1.37[1]	4.51[1]
Split sample	1,538/1,527		12.1/12.3	2.9/2.7	<3–15/<3–15		

Note: For data protection, minimum and maximum scores are given using operators (<) if at least one score below or above the reported minimum/maximum is obtained by fewer than three individuals.

[1] Skewness/kurtosis test for normality significant, $p < 0.05$.

expected substantial ceiling effect at age 4 and an even stronger ceiling effect at age 5. Thus, at ages 4 and 5, this subscale is best interpreted as a measure of slow rhyme development.

Table 10 and Figure 9 present descriptive statistics and histograms for the Print Awareness subscale. This subscale is administered only to 4- and 5-year olds. The items do not change with age, and thus the table and figure demonstrate developmental growth. At age 4 there is no evidence for skewness or a ceiling effect, but by age 5 both are apparent, reflecting major advances in this skill across the population at this age.

Table 11 and Figure 10 present descriptive statistics and a histogram for Letter Knowledge. This subscale is administered only at age 5. Letter knowledge is highly variable in 5-year-old Danish children, with a substantial proportion knowing all letters presented and an almost equally large proportion scoring 0. The shape of the histogram is unusual with its downward trend in the percentage of children as the scores increase and with a dramatic increase in percentage for the maximum score. A similar pattern was seen in an earlier version of the assessment material, with an approximate doubling of the percentage of children who obtained the maximum score of 12 compared to the percentage of children scoring 11. This pattern of scores suggests that letter knowledge may often be learned "in a burst" from modest knowledge to relatively complete knowledge.

Table 12 and Figure 11 present descriptive statistics and a histogram for the Deletion subscale, which is administered only to 5-year-olds. For this subscale, there is a substantial floor effect but also variability, suggesting that this skill is still at an early stage of development at age 5. Recall that the test comprises word-part deletion, syllable deletion, and sound deletion, the latter being the hardest. In a future revision, as well as in adaptations for other languages, floor effects could be minimized by omitting the sound deletion subsection of the test.

3.6.3 Relation of Subscale Scores to Gender and Family Socioeconomic Status

It is well-documented in research that the rate of language development varies as a function of both gender and SES, and this pattern was also found in our sample.

Table 13 shows the gender-related results, gender effect sizes (Cohen's *d*, indicating the percentage of a standard deviation for the gender difference), and significance level at age 3. Girls scored significantly higher than boys on three out of four subscales. Only for Rhyme were the scores for boys and girls virtually identical.

Table 10 Mean scores, standard deviations, range, and distributional characteristics for the subscale Print Awareness for 4- and 5-year-olds. Values for the two split sample groups

Print Awareness	N	Missings	Mean	SD	Range	Skewness	Kurtosis
3-year-olds	-		-	-	-	-	-
4-year-olds	3,621	293	8.1	3.4	0–16	0.02	2.31[1]
Split sample	1,803/1,818		8.1/8.2	3.5/3.4	0–16/0–16	0.06/−0.03	2.26/2.37
5-year-olds	3,109	103	10.9	3.4	0–16	−0.58[1]	1.89[1]
Split sample	1,566/1,543		10.8/11.0	3.4/3.3	0–16/0–16	−0.54/−0.62	2.71/2.89

[1] Skewness/kurtosis test for normality significant, $p < 0.05$.

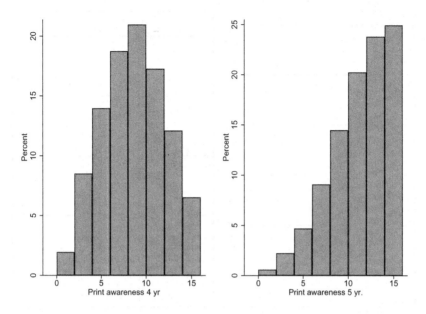

Figure 9 Distribution of scores on the Print Awareness subscale for children aged 4 and 5 years

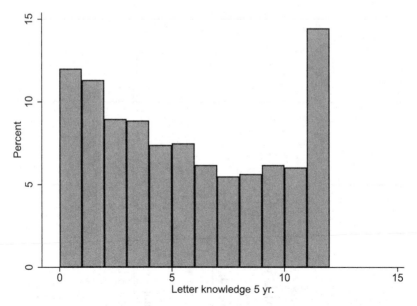

Figure 10 Distribution of scores on the Letter Knowledge subscale for children aged 5 years

Table 11 Mean scores, standard deviations, range, and distributional characteristics for the subscale Letter Knowledge for 5-year-olds. Values for the two split sample groups

Letter Knowledge	N	Missings	Mean	SD	Range	Skewness	Kurtosis
3-year-olds	-	-	-	-	-	-	-
4-year-olds	-	-	-	-	-	-	-
5-year-olds	2,041	1,171	5.2	3.9	0–12	0.29[1]	1.77[1]
Split sample	1,010/1,031		5.1/5.4	4.0/3.9	0–12/0–12	0.32/0.26	1.78/1.76

[1] Skewness/kurtosis test for normality significant, $p < 0.05$.

Table 12 Mean scores, standard deviations, range, and distributional characteristics for the subscale Deletion for 5-year-olds. Values for the two split sample groups

Deletion	N	Missings	Mean	SD	Range	Skewness	Kurtosis
3-year-olds	-	-	-	-	-	-	-
4-year-olds	-	-	-	-	-	-	-
5-year-olds	1,852	1,360	6.0	4.3	0–15	0.21[1]	1.89[1]
Split sample	911/941		6.0/5.9	4.2/4.4	0–15/0–15	0.22/0.20	1.96/1.83

[1] Skewness/kurtosis test for normality significant, $p < 0.05$.

Table 13 Mean scores (SDs) for 3-year-old boys and girls, effect size, and significance of the gender difference on each subscale

Age 3	Boys		Girls			
Subscale	*N*	*M*	*N*	*M*	*d*	*p*
Vocabulary	1,870	10.4 (5.2)	1,743	11.7 (5.4)	0.23	.001
Comprehension	1,938	13.4 (3.3)	1,784	13.8 (3.3)	0.13	.001
Communication	1,437	37.8 (8.8)	1,332	39.2 (8.7)	0.15	.001
Rhyme	1,381	7.2 (3.1)	1,342	7.3 (3.4)	0.02	.532

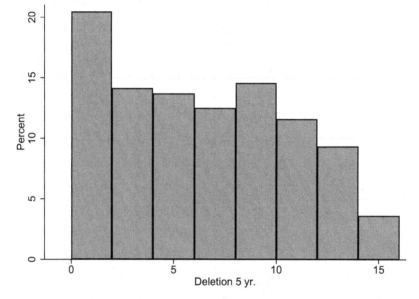

Figure 11 Distribution of scores on the Deletion subscale for children aged 5 years

At 4 years old, the girls scored significantly higher than the boys on all of the subscales with the largest effect size for Communication and the smallest effect size for Rhyme; see Table 14.

At 5 years old, the girls again scored significantly higher than the boys on all of the subscales with the largest effect size for Letter Knowledge and the smallest effect size for the Deletion subscale; see Table 15.

In summary, at each age assessed here, girls are, on average, more advanced in their language and preliteracy development than boys. The gender difference is least pronounced for skills related to phonological awareness, namely rhyme skills and word-part deletion skills, but it is still significant, with the exception

Table 14 Mean scores (SDs) for 4-year-old boys and girls, effect size, and significance of the gender difference on each subscale

Age 4	Boys		Girls			
Subscale	*N*	*M*	*N*	*M*	*d*	*p*
Vocabulary	1,950	13.6 (4.9)	1,828	14.5 (4.6)	0.19	0.001
Comprehension	1,997	14.2 (2.9)	1,874	14.8 (2.8)	0.21	0.001
Communication	1,380	43. (8.1)	1,296	45.6 (7.9)	0.33	0.001
Rhyme	1,834	9.9 (3.5)	1,748	10.3 (3.7)	0.09	0.006
Print awareness	1,832	7.7 (3.4)	1,778	8.6 (3.4)	0.25	0.001

Table 15 Mean scores (SDs) for 5-year-old boys and girls, effect size, and significance of the gender difference on each subscale

Age 5		Boys		Girls			
Subscale	*N*	*M*	*N*	*M*	*d*	*p*
Vocabulary	1,599	14.3 (4.4)	1,535	15.1 (4.2)	0.17	0.001
Comprehension	1,621	14.3 (2.9)	1,559	15.2 (2.7)	0.31	0.001
Communication	1,104	46.0 (8.4)	1,019	48.4 (8.0)	0.30	0.001
Rhyme	1,550	12.0 (2.9)	1,509	12.4 (2.7)	0.18	0.001
Print Awareness	1,571	10.5 (3.4)	1,532	11.3 (3.2)	0.26	0.001
Letter Knowledge	1,050	4.5 (3.8)	987	6.1 (3.9)	0.42	0.001
Deletion	949	5.7 (4.3)	900	6.2 (4.3)	0.14	0.002

of rhyme skills, in 3-year-olds. Given that boys seem to catch up with girls at later ages (Wallentin, 2009), we have chosen to establish separate norms for boys and girls in order not to over-identify boys (false positives, assigned to either special intervention or focused intervention) and under-identify girls (false negatives, assigned to general intervention) with language impairment or delayed language development.

To assess the degree to which language and preliteracy scores were related to parental SES, we correlated scores with maternal education, paternal education, and household income for each of the three ages. The results are shown in Tables 16, 17, and 18, one table for each age. This analysis serves as a tentative validation of the subtests, given that early language development is typically found to be related to family SES (Fernald et al., 2013; Hoff, 2006; Huttenlocher et al., 2010). These relations have also been found to hold for Danish using an earlier version of the present instrument on a different sample (Højen et al., 2021).

Table 16 Zero-order correlation (with 95% CIs) between parental SES variables and language and preliteracy outcomes for 3-year-olds (*N* = 2,258–3,596)

Subscale	Maternal education	Paternal education	Household income
Vocabulary	0.24 (0.21–0.27)	0.21 (0.18–0.25)	0.11 (0.07–0.14)
Comprehension	0.18 (0.15–0.21)	0.19 (0.16–0.24)	0.10 (0.07–0.13)
Communication	0.19 (0.16–0.23)	0.17 (0.13–0.21)	0.09 (0.06–0.13)
Rhyme	0.17 (0.12–0.20)	0.15 (0.11–0.19)	0.06 (0.03–0.10)

Note: All correlations were significant at *p* < 0.001, except for Rhyme correlated with Household Income, *p* = 0.001.

Table 17 Zero-order correlation (with 95% CIs) between parental SES variables and language and preliteracy outcomes for 4-year-olds (*N* = 2,266–3,910)

Subscale	Maternal education	Paternal education	Household income
Vocabulary	0.22 (0.19–0.25)	0.18 (0.15–0.22)	0.09 (0.05–0.12)
Comprehension	0.19 (0.16–0.22)	0.14 (0.10–0.17)	0.07 (0.03–0.10)
Communication	0.14 (0.10–0.17)	0.14 (0.09–0.18)	0.09 (0.05–0.13)
Rhyme	0.20 (0.17–0.24)	0.19 (0.15–0.22)	0.11 (0.08–0.14)
Print awareness	0.19 (0.16–0.22)	0.17 (0.13–0.20)	0.11 (0.08–0.14)

Note: All correlations were significant at *p* < 0.001.

Table 18 Zero-order correlation (with 95% CIs) between parental SES variables and language and preliteracy outcomes for 5-year-olds (*N* = 1,534–3,208)

Subscale	Maternal education	Paternal education	Household income
Vocabulary	0.20 (0.17–0.23)	0.15 (0.11–0.19)	0.10 (0.07–0.14)
Comprehension	0.17 (0.14–0.20)	0.13 (0.09–0.17)	0.05 (0.02–0.09)
Communication	0.16 (0.12–0.20)	0.14 (0.09–0.19)	0.13 (0.09–0.17)
Rhyme	0.18 (0.15–0.21)	0.20 (0.17–0.24)	0.14 (0.11–0.18)
Print Awareness	0.17 (0.14–0.20)	0.15 (0.11–0.19)	0.12 (0.08–0.15)
Letter Knowledge	0.18 (0.14–0.22)	0.22 (0.18–0.27)	0.11 (0.06–0.15)
Deletion	0.12 (0.07–0.17)	0.12 (0.07–0.17)	0.05 (0.00–0.09)

Note: All correlations were significant at *p* < 0.001, except for Deletion correlated with Household Income, *p* = 0.039.

At all ages, each of the SES variables was significantly correlated with each of the language and preliteracy outcomes. Among the SES variables, the strongest correlations were with maternal education and paternal education and the weakest was with household income; the confidence intervals indicate that the correlation with household income was significantly weaker in most cases.

3.7 Psychometric Qualities of the Instrument

The gold standard in terms of the diagnostic validity of an assessment instrument such as the present one (and *LA 2* as well) is a high association between being referred for extra intervention and actually requiring extra intervention – over and above the usual instructional activities in ECEC centers – as determined by speech-language professionals. However, we do not have clinical evaluation data for children in the norming sample to compare with, which would have allowed us to determine the strength of the association between actually requiring intervention and having received low scores on the language assessment (percentiles 1–5 or 11–15); in other words, we cannot determine the sensitivity and specificity of the instruments. We know a priori, of course, that sensitivity and specificity will vary with the cut-off points. If the cut-off point for *special intervention* were percentile 10 rather than percentile 5, sensitivity would go up and specificity would go down. However, it is an important future study to conduct to determine the sensitivity and specificity of both *LA 3–6* and *LA 2*. This will have to be done in collaboration with Danish municipalities, with which children's language assessment data reside and which also make the decision to provide language intervention to children.

3.7.1 Internal Consistency

In spite of pilot testing of the subscales during development, they are unlikely to be perfect. With the much larger norming sample compared to the pilot samples, we can get a better evaluation of internal consistency. To determine internal consistency, Cronbach's alpha coefficients for the subscales for each age group are shown in Table 19 and, in addition, item-total correlations, which indicate the correlation between an individual item and the total score without that item. The alpha values were generally high, indicating high internal consistency. The exception to this is the Comprehension subscale for age 4 and age 5, with alphas of 0.67 and 0.68, respectively. Accordingly, the item-total correlation ranges for that scale are relatively low, but no specific items seem to be dragging the alphas down. However, in future revisions, items from the low end of the range of item-total correlations will have to be replaced. This, of course, will require substantial pilot testing to be sure that the substituted items contribute to higher internal consistency.

Table 19 Cronbach's alpha and item-total correlation range for each subscale for each age group

Subscale	Age 3 $N = 2,730$–$3,734$		Age 4 $N = 2,686$–$3,884$		Age 5 $N = 1,852$–$3,186$	
	Alpha	Item-total	Alpha	Item-total	Alpha	Item-total
Vocabulary	0.87	0.34–0.60	0.84	0.35–0.56	0.82	0.32–0.56
Comprehension	0.78	0.30–0.52	0.67	0.24–0.49	0.68	0.27–0.46
Communication	0.94	0.53–0.84	0.93	0.55–0.85	0.94	0.61–0.83
Rhyme	0.95	0.33–0.60	0.88	0.35–0.61	0.89	0.38–0.64
Print Awareness			0.79	0.32–0.61	0.79	0.32–0.61
Letter Knowledge					0.89	0.58–0.75
Deletion					0.89	0.37–0.74

Table 20 Zero-order correlations (with 95% CIs) between subscales for 3-year-olds ($N = 2,730$–$3,734$)

Subscale	1	2	3
1 Rhyme	-		
2 Comprehension	0.34 (0.66–0.70)	-	
3 Vocabulary	0.42 (0.39–0.45)	0.68 (0.66–0.70)	-
4 Communication	0.25 (0.21–0.29)	0.45 (0.42–0.48)	0.50 (0.47–0.53)

Note: All correlations were significant at $p < 0.001$.

3.7.2 Construct Validity

To evaluate overall construct validity for the entire instrument, we first calculated zero-order correlations between all subscales separately for each age group. As outlined in Section 3.5.1, the results report summarizes the subscales in two summary scores; that is, oral language skills (Vocabulary, Comprehension, Communication) and preliteracy skills (Rhyme, Print Awareness, Letter Knowledge, Deletion). The zero-order correlations also help evaluate the extent to which these conceptually defined summary scores were empirically consistent; as a second step in this evaluation, we estimated structural equation models (confirmatory factor analyses), again separately for each age.

Tables 20–22 show the zero-order correlations between all subscales. It is notable that Vocabulary generally has the highest correlations with the widest range of other measures. Specifically, the correlation between Vocabulary and Comprehension was significantly stronger than other correlations, judging by

Table 21 Zero-order correlations (with 95% CIs) between all subscales for 4-year-olds (N = 2,451–3,884)

Subscale	1	2	3	4
1 Rhyme	-			
2 Print Awareness	0.39 (0.36–0.41)	-		
3 Comprehension	0.41 (0.39–0.44)	0.45 (0.42–0.47)	-	
4 Vocabulary	0.49 (0.47–0.52)	0.51 (0.48–0.53)	0.60 (0.58–0.62)	-
5 Communication	0.31 (0.27–0.34)	0.38 (0.35–0.41)	0.37 (0.34–0.40)	0.47 (0.44–0.50)

Note: All correlations were significant at $p < 0.001$.

Table 22 Zero-order correlations (with 95% CIs) between all subscales and for 5-year-olds (*N* = 1,800–3,186)

Subscale	1	2	3	4	5	6
1 Rhyme	-					
2 Print Awareness	0.39 (0.36–0.42)	-				
3 Letter Naming	0.37 (0.33–0.40)	0.42 (0.38–0.46)	-			
4 Deletion	0.41 (0.37–0.45)	0.46 (0.42–0.50)	0.40 (0.36–0.44)	-		
5 Comprehension	0.43 (0.40–0.46)	0.46 (0.43–0.49)	0.33 (0.29–0.37)	0.43 (0.39–0.46)	-	
6 Vocabulary	0.42 (0.39–0.45)	0.51 (0.48–0.54)	0.38 (0.34–0.42)	0.45 (0.41–0.48)	0.56 (0.53–0.58)	-
7 Communication	0.31 (0.27–0.35)	0.32 (0.29–0.36)	0.33 (0.29–0.37)	0.33 (0.29–0.37)	0.34 (0.30–0.38)	0.40 (0.36–0.43)

Note: All correlations were significant at *p* < 0.001.

the confidence intervals of correlation coefficients. This suggests that vocabulary is a core skill that is broadly indicative of general language development and should be included in all language assessment instruments that target broad language skills and not just a specific language skill such as phonological awareness.

Focusing on the two summary score constructs, oral language (Comprehension, Vocabulary, Communication) and preliteracy skills (Rhyme, Print Awareness, Letter Naming, Deletion), the correlations between subscales within each construct were generally of similar magnitudes to the correlations between subscales across the two constructs, although slightly higher on average within than across constructs. This raises a question about how separate these theoretically defined constructs really are.

To further examine the extent to which the oral language and preliteracy constructs represent separate factors, we estimated structural equation models for 4-year-olds and 5-year-olds separately. Note that for 3-year-olds, there is just one preliteracy subscale, Rhyme. Also note that the number of subscales administered to 4- and 5-year-olds differs. The models were estimated in Stata using maximum likelihood with missing values and standardized coefficients and values.

Figure 12 shows structural equation models of how the subscales relate to the oral language construct and the preliteracy construct for 4-year-olds and 5-year-olds. Post-estimation of the model fit indicated good fits: Significant chi-square fit indices for both 4-year-olds ($\chi^2 = 68.7$, $p < 0.001$) and 5-year-olds ($\chi^2 = 13.4$, $p < 0.001$), which is not uncommon in larger samples (Bentler & Bonett, 1980), but a low root mean squared error of approximation (4-year-olds: 0.024; 5-year-olds: 0.037) and high comparative fit indices (4-year-olds: 0.995; 5-year-olds: 0.982) and high Tucker-Lewis indices (4-year-olds: 0.995; 5-year-olds: 0.982). The subscales were loaded significantly on each construct for both ages ($ps < 0.001$). There was significant positive covariance between the two summary score constructs ($p < 0.001$).

Summing up, the good model fits suggest that the conceptually defined constructs are reasonable (though also with a high degree of covariance between the constructs), whereas the similarity of the strengths of pairwise correlations within and across the two constructs suggests that the conceptually defined constructs may not fully reflect genuinely distinct constructs, with the exception of generally strong correlations between the language subscales, Vocabulary and Comprehension. This, in turn, suggests that a total summary score might work just as well and that educators should look at scores on individual subscales to determine areas of language development that need support in that particular child.

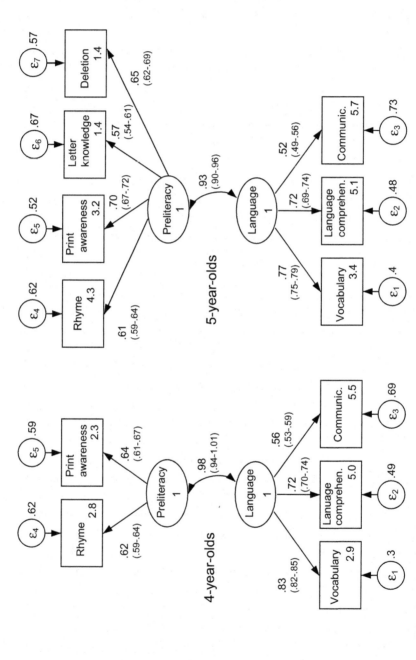

Figure 12 Structural equation model of the loadings of subscales on the two summary score constructs for 4-year-olds, left, and for 5-year-olds, right. Goodness of fit for each model was $R = 0.84$ (4-year-olds) and $R = 0.87$ (5-year-olds)

3.7.3 External Validity

As there is no gold standard language measure in Denmark, it was not possible to perform an external validation study for all subscales. The external validity of *LA 3–6* could only be compared with Danish adaptations of the Peabody Picture Vocabulary Test, 4th edition (PPVT-4; Dunn & Dunn, 2007) and the Expressive Vocabulary Test, 2nd edition (EVT-2; Williams, 2007). A sample of 133 3–6-year-old children, approximately equally distributed across age groups, participated in this study. Correlations between the instruments are presented in Table 23. Five children did not complete the external tests.

The concurrent correlations of *LA 3–6* subscales with PPVT-4 ranged from 0.33 to 0.57 and were highest for Vocabulary, Comprehension, and Print Awareness and lowest for Rhyme. Correlations with the EVT-2 ranged from 0.10 to 0.42 and were highest for Vocabulary and Comprehension. The correlations with the preliteracy subscales were weak. It is noteworthy that the *LA 3–6* Productive Vocabulary subscale correlated more strongly with the PPVT-4, which is a receptive vocabulary test, than with the EVT-2, which is a productive vocabulary test. One possible reason for this is a higher tendency for ceiling effects for EVT-2 than for PPVT-4. One might also speculate that the PPVT-4 has higher reliability than the EVT-2, but this is probably not the case; for the English versions, test-retest reliability is slightly higher for the EVT-2 (0.94–0.97) than for the PPVT-4 (0.87–0.93) (Pearson, 2007).

3.7.4 Procedure for Establishing Percentile Scores

The results of the language assessment are reported as percentile scores. The instrument assigns percentile scores on each subscale to children based on their raw score. For this purpose, we developed percentile norms from the representative

Table 23 Zero-order correlations (with 95% CIs) between subscales of *LA 3–6* and EVT-2 and PPVT-4 for children aged 3–5

Subtest		EVT-2		PPVT-4	
	N	*r*	*p*	*r*	*p*
Rhyme	128	0.18 (0.01–0.34)	0.042	0.33 (0.17–0.48)	0.001
Print Awareness	95	0.15 (−.0.05–0.34)	0.147	0.49 (0.32–0.63)	0.001
Letter Naming	65	0.33 (0.09–0.53)	0.007	0.39 (0.16–0.58)	0.001
Deletion	64	0.29 (0.05–0.50)	0.020	0.42 (0.19–0.60)	0.001
Comprehension	128	0.39 (0.23–0.53)	0.001	0.57 (0.44–0.68)	0.001
Vocabulary	128	0.42 (0.27–0.55)	0.001	0.55 (0.42–0.66)	0.001

norming sample. The percentile score corresponding to a raw score value x of a child at age a (in months) is based on all children of the same gender and with an age of +/− 4 months and tested with the same material. For these children, an indicator variable is created indicating whether the child has a score of x or less. Then a logistic regression is fitted in these children with age as the only covariate, and the prediction from this model is recorded. The percentile score is then defined as the average between the predictions obtained for the values x and x−1. Percentile scores above 99 are set to 99. As noted in Section 3.5.1, the subscale raw scores were standardized and averaged to generate the oral language summary score and the preliteracy summary score. These summary scores were, in turn, converted to percentile scores.

The procedure of considering the ages +/− 4 months means that we "borrow data strength" from ages just above and below the age in question. The purpose was to iron out natural fluctuations that cause anomalies in the normative development. For example, it happened regularly that a particular age group, such as 39-month-olds, would have a mean score on a subscale that was lower than the mean score of 40-month-olds. We have no reason to assume a drop in skills from one month to the next, although conceivable; it is much more likely that such a drop occurred in the norming study through sampling error – for example, if our group of 39-month-olds had slightly higher skills than our 40-month-olds and therefore obtained higher scores. By considering neighboring ages using the above procedure, such bumps in age-score relations were ironed out in most cases. In a few cases, however, anomalies persisted, meaning that, for example, a 40-month-old could obtain a higher percentile score than a 39-month-old from the same raw score. In future updates of the *LA 3–6*, we plan to manually eradicate such anomalies, as is also done for *LA 2* (see Section 4.9.5), on the assumption that language development does not go backwards – at least not in predictable steps, let alone in predictable steps for predictable monthly ages.

4 A Language Assessment Instrument for 2-Year-Olds

4.1 Background

As mentioned earlier, according to Danish legislation, children aged 3 must be language assessed if any language development delay is suspected. As of 2018, Danish municipalities are also authorized to assess children suspected of language delays at an even earlier age in order to initiate language development support as soon as possible in the ECEC centers and by instructing parents in how to best support their child's language development.

Growing research evidence demonstrates that children's language skills at or even before age 2 are predictive of later educational outcomes

(Bleses et al., 2016; Lee, 2011). However, as also clear from, for example, Bleses et al. (2016), measures of language skills at age 2 are not highly accurate predictors of later literacy skills on an individual level. This could be due to some children being late bloomers or due to greater measurement error in early measures. Still, a language assessment instrument for 2-year-olds was commissioned by the Danish Board of Social Affairs. The intention was that with this instrument, *LA 2*, Danish ECEC centers should be able to assess child language development even earlier so that intervention could be provided to children as soon as possible if their language development was slow or otherwise impaired. This can be seen as a way of "erring on the side of caution" by risking over-identifying children who may simply be late bloomers. However, because *LA 2* is designed to generate scores that are comparable with the scores of *LA 3–6*, it is possible to follow up on children's development over time. In this way, it is possible to determine with more data points whether a child with low scores on *LA 2* is a late bloomer or whether the child needs continuing intervention.

The design of *LA 2* was based on the following criteria: The instrument should validly assess children's language development. Two-year-old children should feel safe and comfortable while being assessed. Administration of the assessment should be as simple and take as little time as possible. Proper administration of the assessment should be possible for ECEC professionals who are not speech and language professionals. The instrument should align with *LA 3–6* to facilitate comparable assessment results across the two instruments.

In its development, *LA 2* was based on the same principles as those for *LA 3–6*, notably being research-based, pilot tested, age- and gender-normed on a representative sample, internally and externally validated, and sensitive across the entire distribution of language skills, although with a priority for sensitivity in the low end of the distribution (see Section 3.3).

LA 2 is for children aged 22 to 34 months; thus the age ranges for *LA 2* and *LA 3–6* overlap, and language development can be followed continuously between 22 and 71 months of age.

4.2 Evidence behind the Subscales

In order to ensure that the *LA 2* was based on the most relevant linguistic dimensions, a systematic review was carried out in order to determine which of the very early linguistic dimensions are predictive of children's later language development and related competencies; our review was a subproject of a more comprehensive review of risk factors for educational outcomes (Bleses, Hvidman, et al., 2018). For the present purpose, we reanalyzed the data from the original review to focus on the predictive relations of skills at around age 2 to skills during school ages. Specifically, we asked: (1) which language skills at around age 2 have been examined in empirical studies for their relation to later reading, math, and social skills in kindergarten, grades 1–6, and grades 7–10, and (2) among the language skills examined at around age 2, which ones show predictive relations to reading, math, and social skills in kindergarten, grades 1–6, and grades 7–10?

In the original review, 129 studies were included, based on a search protocol, which examined the relation of early oral language skills to later skills. Studies were included only if they had at least two measures; at least one of them was required to be an early preschool-age measure and at least one was required to be a later school-age measure. Because our aim was to examine early language measures as predictors, we required the early measures to focus on *specific* language dimensions. That is, we excluded studies that examined composite measures of, for example, expressive language (which might include measures of both vocabulary and grammar). We also excluded studies examining meta-linguistic awareness or phonological awareness, which are difficult to examine in 2-year-olds and which would therefore be unlikely to be examined reliably by educators who do not have professional training in speech and language development and assessment.

Early skills that were examined included vocabulary, morphology/syntax (grammar for short), and language comprehension. Later skills included the just-mentioned early skills and additionally word decoding, reading comprehension, reading in general (including several components), math, social skills, and emotional/behavioral skills.

Twelve studies examined oral skills at age 2 and correlated these skills with later skills. One study was from Denmark while the remaining eleven studies were from the US, Europe, or South or Central America. The studies differed considerably in sample size. Some were small-scale studies focusing on late talkers at age 2; for example, Rescorla (2005). Others were larger-scale population-based studies; for example, Poll and Miller (2013). The twelve studies are listed in the Appendix.

Addressing our first question, we identified three language skills that have been examined at around age 2 and have also had their correlations with later skills examined. Those three skills were vocabulary, language comprehension, and grammar. Vocabulary has been examined much more often – fifty-four times – than comprehension, seven times, or grammar, six times.

To address our second question, we then examined the results of these studies to determine whether there were significant pairwise predictive relations between early and later skills. Table 24 shows the proportion of positive correlations of vocabulary with later measures. Vocabulary generally correlates

Table 24 Percentage of 54 identified correlations that are significantly positive between vocabulary at age 2 and later academic skills in grade 0, grades 1–6, and grades 7–10

Skill	Grade 0		Grades 1–6		Grades 7–10	
	k	**% positive correlations**	**k**	**% positive correlations**	**k**	**% positive correlations**
Lang. comprehen.	1	100	1	100	-	-
Grammar	-	-	-	-	1	100
Oral language skills	2	100	-	-	-	-
Reading comprehen.	6	100	6	100	3	67
Decoding/reading	7	29	6	17	3	33
Writing/spelling	4	50	4	50	1	0
Math	5	100	1	100	-	-
Social skills	1	100	-	-	-	-
Self-regulation	2	50	-	-	-	-

Note: k indicates the number of studies.

with all later measures at some point in most studies, including skills that are not directly language-based, such as math, social skills, and self-regulation. Only later decoding/reading measures were relatively seldom correlated with early vocabulary scores. In addition, the percentage of significant correlations with early vocabulary scores decreases in the higher grades; that is, with a greater distance in time between the two measures.

For correlations of language comprehension at around age 2 with later vocabulary or reading skills, only one of the seven identified studies showed significant relations. Correlations of grammar skills at around age 2 with later skills were significant in only two out of six identified studies (one time with later reading and one time with later math skills).

In summary, the systematic review points to early vocabulary as clearly the most promising early measure for predicting later skills. However, it should also be noted that the number of different early skills that have been examined for prediction is very limited, so other yet unexamined early measures could show important predictive correlations with later skills.

4.3 Content

Because of the importance of vocabulary for the prediction of later skills summarized in Section 4.2, it was deemed essential to examine both receptive and productive (or expressive) vocabulary. For receptive vocabulary, the assessment battery adapted the CCT – Computerized Comprehension Task (Friend & Keplinger, 2008; Friend et al., 2012).

For productive vocabulary, we used an existing instrument, namely the *CDI: Educator* (Bleses, Jensen, et al., 2018). This instrument also included a scale assessing decontextualized language use. It was decided to include this scale in the *LA 2* battery, partly because it was included in the original *CDI: Educator* and partly because at this early stage of development of *LA 2*, it was desirable to explore other possible early predictors. This was also part of the reason for including the fourth subscale, which was pragmatic communication skills as evaluated by the educator. Another part of the reason for the inclusion of pragmatics was feedback from educators and speech professionals who voiced the opinion that it was important to assess more general communication skills in children who might not have a large vocabulary but who might be very well able to communicate using other or more general means.

In summary, the *LA 2* consists of four subscales. Only one of them, Receptive Vocabulary, is a test in which the child participates. The decision to have only one direct test was based on a desire to minimize the requirements expected of the child. The remaining three subscales are checklists that are filled in by the

Table 25 Subscales of *LA 2*

Subscale	Assessment type	Items
Receptive vocabulary	Test	39
Productive vocabulary	Checklist	70
Decontextualized language use	Checklist	5
Communicative skills	Checklist	23

child's usual professional ECEC educator. Filling in the checklists requires experience with the child's language use in day-to-day interaction. Beyond minimizing the requirements expected of the child, it has the advantage of being based on much more experience than a single test session, as discussed in the introduction, and knowing that children may vary in test-taking ability. Table 25 gives an overview of the instrument.

4.4 Development of the Four Subscales

4.4.1 Development of the Receptive Vocabulary Test

As mentioned, we adapted an existing American computer-based test of receptive vocabulary (the CCT; Friend & Keplinger, 2008; Friend et al., 2012). In this test, children are shown two pictures at a time on a touch screen – for example, a pacifier and a teddy bear – and an adult asks the child to touch one of them; for example, the pacifier. In our adaptation of the CCT, the administrator – with live voice – also asks the child to touch or point to one of two pictures. But our adaptation differs in several ways from the CCT.

An initial change compared to the original CCT concerned stimulus presentation and child response mode. In the original CCT, the pictures are onscreen, and responses are recorded automatically when the child touches a picture within a specified frame on the touch screen. In our adaptation, children point to a picture in a booklet showing the target picture and the foil side by side. This change was in part due to the desire of the commissioning body, the Ministry for Children and Education, for the test situation to resemble shared book reading in order to minimize stress or insecurity in the child. In addition, in a previous Danish iPad-based adaptation of the CCT, which the authors made for a randomized controlled trial of language intervention in 1–2-year-olds, children were reported to often have difficulties touching the pictures illustrated in such a way that the iPad successfully recorded the response. Observed errors in touch included sliding, touching with multiple fingers, or touching too hard or too long, all of which could result in failure to record the response or even shutting down the app.

The above difficulties can be avoided by using a picture book. However, the use of pointing to a picture in a book as a task response has its own challenges. It is not always obvious whether the child has pointed or not. A child may shift their gaze to a picture and even say "There!" without clearly pointing their finger. Our decision, to minimize judgment by the educators, was to instruct them to only record a response if the child clearly points with their hand or finger. The instructions also give suggestions as to how to elicit this type of response from the child.

A second major change from the CCT was to develop separate but overlapping difficulty levels for children under 2 years (i.e., 22–23 months), children aged 2–2½ years (24–29 months), and children over 2½ years (30–34 months). One reason for this was to avoid floor effects in the youngest children and ceiling effects in the oldest children, a particular concern given the expanded age range compared to the CCT, by adding easier and harder words. We also wanted to keep the test relatively short so as not to exceed the general attention span of toddlers. This precluded the inclusion of several additional words to a fixed list for all children as a means to avoid floor and ceiling effects with the expanded age range.

The words chosen for the test were, for a start, the Danish equivalents of the words of the original CCT. To expand the word list with easier as well as harder words, the norms for words of the Danish receptive CDI were used as a source of information on how widely specific words are known by Danish children in the age range of 22–34 months.

As in the original CCT, we aimed for three difficulty levels of words: easy, medium-hard, and hard (thirteen each within each age-dependent version). The words used in the three age-dependent versions overlapped so that, roughly, words that are hard in the 22–23 months version are used as medium-hard words in the 24–29 months version and as easy words in the 30–34 months version. Likewise, words that are medium-hard in the 22–23 months version are easy in the 24–29 months version and words that are hard in the 24–29 months version are medium-hard in the 30–34 months version. Easy words in the 22–23 months version and hard words in the 30–34 months version are not used in other versions. In each age-dependent version, easy, medium-hard, and hard words are mixed together so that children experience random variation in difficulty level, with the intention to minimize fatigue due to being unable to respond or finding the task too easy.

Easy words (e.g., *doll*) were expected to be familiar to most children in the age range, while hard words (e.g., *parachute*) were expected to be familiar to few children. These expectations were tested in pilot tests, and the set of items for each version was altered in order to increase or decrease the difficulty level with the aim of obtaining a close to normal distribution of scores. In addition, given the small size and unknown representativeness of the pilot study sample, the choice of words also took into account the above-mentioned CDI data, which were obtained from more than 6,000 children.

It should also be noted that the target words are elicited by showing pictures, and therefore the difficulty of an item is not solely based on how well the child knows a word but also on how well the child can relate the word to the picture. This may vary across children depending on their individual life experiences, but it is also inherently easier to unambiguously illustrate, for example, *penguin* than *park* because parks are more diverse and come in many more shapes and sizes than penguins do, or because a child may relate the word *park* to a specific park (while being unlikely to be familiar with individual penguins).

The composition of the thirty-nine items reflects natural vocabulary development such that in the youngest version, the majority of words are concrete nouns with only a few adjectives or verbs, whereas in the oldest version, the proportion of adjectives and verbs is higher.

4.4.2 Productive Vocabulary and Language Use Subscales

As mentioned in Section 4.3, the entire Productive Vocabulary and the (decontextualized) Language Use scales were taken from an existing instrument, namely the *CDI: Educator* (Bleses, Jensen, et al., 2018). The Productive Vocabulary scale is based on educator report of which words on a word list are known by the child according to the educator's knowledge of the child from day-to-day interactions; that is, words that the educator believes they have heard the child produce. The *CDI: Educator* is a shortened educator version of the Danish version (Bleses et al., 2008a) of the MacArthur-Bates Communicative Development Inventories (Fenson et al., 2007). The scale consists of seventy words, and the same scale is used independently of the child's age (22–34 months). The words are semantically organized in categories, as shown in Table 26.

The *CDI: Educator* instrument has an additional scale consisting of five questions pertaining to decontextualized language use; for example, whether the child speaks about past or future events, speaks about people not present, or relates items to a person not present (for example, "Michael's teddy!"). As noted earlier, this scale became part of *LA 2* as well.

4.4.3 Development of the Communication Subscale

The Communication subscale was partly a new development and partly based on the Communication subscale for *LA 3–6*. The purpose of this scale is to capture a range of pragmatic communication skills, starting from the very basic skills of 2-year-old children who are either beginning to learn Danish as an additional

Table 26 Word examples from the Productive Vocabulary subscale. Adapted from Table 1 of Bleses, Jensen, et al. (2018)

Word category	Items	Examples
Sound effects and animal sounds	2	Ouch, woof-woof
Words for animals and things	4	Car, ball, shoe
Food and drink	4	Ice cream, milk, apple
Body parts	8	Ankle, finger, teeth
Small household items, furniture and rooms, and places to go	13	Paper, drawer, window
People and routines	6	Dad, no, thank you
Action words	21	Dance, help, think
Descriptive words	10	Soft, slow, angry
Particles	2	Each, because

language or who for other reasons have only very basic Danish communication skills. The scale items increase in difficulty to advanced communication skills.

For each item, a "scene" is set, and the educator is asked to use their experience to judge how likely it is that a child would typically produce a target response/behavior. Below are three examples of communicative skills ranging from basic to advanced.

Basic: You are talking to the child while changing a diaper or during a meal. Behavior: The child keeps eye contact with you for at least five seconds at a time.

Medium: The child is playing or eating with other children or adults. Behavior: The child uses words to comment on what is happening without being prompted.

Advanced: The child has heard you tell a story, and the child is retelling that story to another child. Behavior: The child tells the story with enough information and organization that the other child can understand the main points.

The subscale was pilot tested with 100 2-year-olds, and clear ceiling effects were present. Therefore, additional items from the Communication subscale of *LA 3–6* were successfully added to increase difficulty (see Section 4.8).

4.5 Administration

For the administration of *LA 2*, the materials shown in Table 27 were developed. All materials were developed for paper format but have been integrated into IT platforms such as those for *LA 3–6* by commercial as well as governmental suppliers, the latter offering the platform free of charge.

Table 27 Overview of which materials are used for which parts of the assessment process

Material	Administration	Results	Interpretation	Intervention
Assessment form	✓			
Picture booklet	✓			
Results report (IT system)		✓	✓	✓
Supplementary questions to parents			✓	
Manual		✓		

4.5.1 Assessment Form

The assessment form includes all subscales and their associated test items. For each subscale there is a brief guide containing a description of the subscale, information about which materials are to be used, a description of how to perform the Receptive Vocabulary assessment with the child, and information about how to fill out the Productive Vocabulary, Language Use, and Communication subscales, as well as how all subscales are scored. The child's response may be manually recorded on paper and subsequently entered into the IT system, or it can be registered directly in the IT system. This requires that the assessor has a computer or tablet at hand; feedback from users during pilot tests indicates that some experience is required to use a computer/tablet for registering the child's response while at the same time keeping a full focus on the child to keep them engaged in the tasks and facilitate their participation while at the same time not helping them too much.

The language assessment instrument can be administered to all children in ECEC; that is, including bilingual children, although only Danish is assessed. For bilingual children, special care must be taken when interpreting the results (see Section 4.6.3). For children not in ECEC, only the test of receptive vocabulary can be administered because completion of the other three subscales requires ECEC educators' experience with the child's language use in the ECEC center.

4.5.2 Assessment of the Child on Each Subscale

The administration of the Receptive Vocabulary subscale is described here in a little more detail than the subscales of the *LA 3–6* earlier in this Element (as well as for the remaining subscales of *LA 2*, which do not involve the child).

This is because consistency and fidelity in the administration of a test is even more important in the case of very young children.

For the Receptive Vocabulary test, the child is shown two photos next to each other in each of thirty-nine trials. The child's task is to point out, for example, a *sock*. The *foil* (a jacket in Figure 13) is a photo that has a level of difficulty similar to that of the target and additionally – as far as possible – shares some characteristic features (for example, being animals, pieces of clothing, items found in the home, items to put in the mouth, etc.), but priority was given to similarity of difficulty (based on scores for each item on CDI measures; Bleses et al., 2008a), which meant that a few items had word pairs with relatively low content similarity, such as *balloon–bike*.

The educator is advised to ask for the target immediately when showing the two photos in order that the child does not get too interested in one particular photo, which could make it difficult to determine whether the child pointed based on the question or based on their interest in the photo.

The question for the child is phrased slightly differently depending on whether the target word is a noun, a verb, or an adjective. Nouns: *Point to the sock!* (*Where is the sock?*) Verbs: *Point to the one that is jumping!* (*Who is jumping?*) Adjectives: *Point to the one that is tall!* (*Which one is tall?*) The child may be asked up to three times in slightly different ways as deemed appropriate by the educator to help the child understand the question.

Before the thirty-nine test items, four practice items are administered to teach the child what the task is. If the child does not know what to do, the

Figure 13 Example of target (*sock*) and foil (*jacket*) used in the Receptive Vocabulary test

educator may help the child a single time during the practice by pointing and saying in a lively voice, for example, *Theeeere is the baby!* If the child correctly points to two out of the four practice items, the test proper is given. If not, the four practice items are repeated, and once again, the requirement is two correct practice items in order to start the test proper. If this requirement is not met, the test session is aborted and should be taken up again after a few days. If the child still does not pass the practice items, it is up to the educator decide when to try again.

The educator is advised to begin the assessment with a "calm" or "low-key" attitude. If educators are too lively from the beginning, they will run out of "headroom" to turn up the enthusiasm if the child begins to lose interest. Each item is scored depending on whether the child points to the target photo, the foil, or does not point. In practice, only correct responses are counted when tallying the score; the reason for technically distinguishing between the wrong response and no response is to enable the research team to perform follow-up analyses to determine whether wrong and no responses are differentially predictive of later skill development, which is a result that has been found for the CCT, from which this test was derived (Hendrickson et al., 2015; Hendrickson et al., 2017).

The three remaining subscales are in questionnaire form and are completed by an educator who knows the child from day-to-day interaction in the childcare facility. The child is not present, which means that the educators use their knowledge and memory of how the child talks.

The seventy-item Productive Vocabulary subscale is completed by the educators indicating for each word item whether they have heard the child produce the word. The word should be checked off as heard even if the child pronounces it incorrectly but, based on the context, clearly attempted to say the word. If, for example, the educator has heard the child say "lean!" while showing their hands after having washed them, it is likely from the context that the child is saying the word "clean" with a reduced consonant cluster.

A similar approach is used for (decontextualized) language use and for the Communication subscale. The educators use their experience and memory of the child's language use and communication skills in specific concrete, but hypothetical, situations in the everyday (see also Sections 4.4.2 and 4.4.3).

4.6 Results of the Assessment

4.6.1 The Results Report

Just as is the case for *LA 3–6*, the child's performance on *LA 2*, based on the number of items responded to correctly, is to be compared with the age- and gender-specific norms. The resulting report contains a percentile score for each of the subscales just as for *LA 3–6* (see Section 3.5.1). However, because the norming study included only about fifty children per gender per monthly age, percentile scores are given in 5-percentile ranges; giving percentile scores in steps of 1 would suggest a level of precision not warranted, even when data strength was "borrowed" from the ages just above and below the age in question (see Section 4.9.5).

In addition to percentile scores on the individual subscales, a summary percentile score is given. The summary score is generated by standardizing and averaging the individual subscale scores and comparing them to summary scores in the norming sample. A results report similar to that shown in Figure 4 (see Section 3.5.1) for *LA 3–6* is given. Again, the summary score is mainly for administrative and benchmarking purposes, because a child may have specific difficulties in one area of language development but score in the normal range on the summary score. Therefore, educators should focus on the child's results on the individual subscales to determine whether the child is lacking in specific areas of language development.

To generate a summary score across all subscales was a requirement of the Ministry for Children and Education, because many Danish municipalities intend to use such a score either for benchmarking or to track changes between cohorts of children in the face of, for example, new language support initiatives in ECEC centers or changes in the composition of families living in the municipality. It is inherently difficult for municipalities to distinguish the real causes of year-to-year changes or differences between municipalities. For example, one ECEC center/district/municipality may have higher concentrations of at-risk families than another one, and therefore is likely to have children with lower language assessment scores. However, this ECEC center/district/ municipality may actually be doing a better job in terms of supporting children's language development than an ECEC center/district/municipality whose children have higher language assessment scores mainly because of a higher SES demographic. Likewise, demographics can change over time, making year-to-year comparisons potentially difficult to interpret.

4.6.2 Interpretation of Results

The *LA 2* uses the same cut-off points as does *LA 3–6*. Here we summarize the recommendations based on the child's percentile score. We recommend that the lowest-scoring 5 percent of the children should be referred to a professional speech therapist in order to conduct a complete professional speech pathological assessment and potentially to receive specialized intervention. Children with scores from 6th to 15th percentile should be referred to the ECEC centers for focused intervention and a later reevaluation for language delay. Again, it is not in the scope of the instrument and the manual to specify appropriate interventions, but the manual advises work on the specific linguistic weaknesses of a child according to their profile (e.g., low scores on Vocabulary) and gives some examples. The percentile scores for each subscale may help guide educators to focus support on the domains in which the child needs the most help. The remaining 85 percent of the children can be regarded as having language development within the normal range. Thus these children are recommended to continue with the general intervention and the usual instructional activities in the ECEC centers.

4.6.3 Interpretation of Results for Bilingual and Multilingual Children

Just as for *LA 3–6*, the interpretation of the results of *LA 2* for bilingual and multilingual children requires special attention because bilingual children generally have slower language development in each language than do monolingual children, even if the child has been learning both languages from birth. If a child has begun learning Danish as an additional language only a few months before the language assessment, it is obvious that they will be likely to receive very low scores. For children learning Danish primarily in ECEC, we recommend that they are not assessed using *LA 2* if they have spent less than three months in ECEC.

While a bilingual or multilingual child who receives a percentile score within the normal range for monolingual children (percentiles 16–100) is unlikely to have language development problems, low scores (percentiles 1–15) are harder to interpret. A low score can be indicative either of language acquisition problems in general (which would have resulted in a low score in the first language as well, had it been assessed) or limited second-language input and interaction, meaning that the child is highly dominant in the first language. A combination of the two possibilities – developmental problems and lack of second-language input – is possible as well.

In order to help inform the interpretation of the results of bi- and multilingual children, 229 bilingual children were recruited as an addition to the monolingual norming sample. The results showed that bilingual children did not differ from monolingual children uniformly across the four subscales. The ANOVA analyses and effect size estimates indicated that, compared to monolingual children, bilingual children differed particularly in Receptive Vocabulary (bilinguals = 21.5 vs. monolinguals = 29.6, $p < 0.001$, $d = 1.36$), slightly less so in Productive Vocabulary (bilinguals = 21.9 vs. monolinguals

= 40.5, $p < 0.001$, $d = 1.15$), and still slightly less so on decontextualized Language Use (bilinguals = 3.2 vs. monolinguals = 5.7, $p < 0.001$, $d = 0.93$) and the Communication subscale (bilinguals = 30.6 vs. monolinguals = 43.0, $p < 0.001$, $d = 0.93$). The – at least nominally – smaller difference between monolingual and bilingual children in productive rather than receptive vocabulary differs from previous research showing that bilingualism affects productive vocabulary more than receptive vocabulary (Gibson et al., 2012; Gross et al., 2014; Hemsley et al., 2010; Ribot & Hoff, 2014). However, the difference is not easy to interpret because the Receptive Vocabulary scores were obtained from a test whereas the Productive Vocabulary scores were obtained from educator reports. However, taking the differing monolingual-bilingual difference in mean scores between subscales at face value, educators should be less worried when bilingual children receive low scores on the Receptive Vocabulary subscale but more so when they receive low scores on the Language Use and Communication subscales.

In contrast to what was done for *LA 3–6*, we did not develop a set of questions for nonnative parents in order to gain more information about the children's bilingual development. However, the educators are advised to discuss language assessment results with the child's parents in order to help interpret the results, especially if the scores are low. If the parents do not speak Danish to the child in the home, low assessment scores in Danish at this young age are virtually inevitable. On the other hand, if one or both parents, and perhaps siblings, speaks Danish to the child daily and has done so for most of the child's life, very low Danish scores may be a reason for concern. However, given the short time that bilingual 2-year-olds have typically had to acquire the second language, educators are advised to give more attention to bilingual children's Danish-language development *over time* rather than their Danish-language skills at a specific point in time. All else being equal, bilingual children are expected to obtain lower scores than monolingual children. But at the same time, bilingual children should narrow the gap with monolingual children over time. Therefore, it is important to assess low-scoring bilingual children regularly; for example, biannually.

4.7 Norming Study

4.7.1 Sample

To recruit children for the norming study, all ninety-eight Danish municipalities were asked to participate; thirteen municipalities chose to participate. The participants came from 135 ECEC centers and home-based ECEC groups from across Denmark. The municipalities represented geographically disparate

Table 28 Monolingual Danish children in the norming
sample in three age ranges

Age (mon.)	Boys	Girls	Total
22–23	90	92	182
24–29	395	337	732
30–34	249	216	465

parts of Denmark, and there were municipalities with urban profiles as well as rural profiles, and they were thus representative of Danish municipalities.

Table 28 shows the number of monolingual boys and girls in the sample. The children were grouped in three age categories: less than 2 years old (22–23 months), 2 to 2½ years old (24–29 months), and more than 2½ years old (30–34 months). Only children with a Danish (i.e., nonimmigrant and monolingual) background were in the norming sample; as was the case for *LA 3–6*, the purpose was to develop norms for monolingual children. While norms for bilingual and multilingual children would be highly desirable, such norms are extremely difficult to develop because of the multiple factors that may vary within this group of children, as discussed in Section 1.6.

The SES background – as indexed by maternal education – of children in the sample with a Danish background was generally representative of the population, although mothers with high levels of education were slightly overrepresented. When calculating the norms, scores were weighted so as to level the slight SES bias, which, however, made virtually no difference compared with basing norms on unweighted scores (even though SES correlated with the raw scores). However, all scores presented in this Element are raw, unweighted scores. Maternal education levels are shown in Table 29.

4.8 Descriptive Statistics

4.8.1 Descriptive Statistics for All Subscales

Descriptive statistics for the summary scores of the subscales of *LA 2* for each age group – 22–23, 24–29, and 30–34 months old – are shown in Tables 29–35 and Figures 14–17. Although only the Receptive Vocabulary subscale uses different items for the three age groups, the scores and distributions are shown separately for each age group for the other subscales as well in order to illustrate the relationship of age to scores and score distribution. For data protection reasons, minimum and maximum values have been obscured if

Table 29 Maternal educational background for children in
the norming sample

	N	**Proportion %**
Short (basic schooling)	158	11
Short-mid	421	30
Mid-long	404	29
Long (BA or longer)	371	27
Missing	37	3

certain scores have been obtained by fewer than four individuals. Likewise, histogram bins encompass several scores in order not to show scores obtained by fewer than four individuals. As also done for descriptives of *LA 3–6* above, we randomly divided the children into two groups for each age group in order to examine the robustness of the data via split sample results.

Table 30 and Figure 14 present descriptive statistics and histograms for the Receptive Vocabulary subscale. Because there is a change of items across ages for this subscale (Section 4.4.1), the scores are not directly comparable across the age groups. The histograms are more informative, as they demonstrate that variability in this skill is appropriately captured, the degree of skewness is visualized, and any floor or ceiling effects are detected. The distributions are left-skewed, and there is a tendency to a ceiling effect in the 22–23 months age group, although few children obtained the two highest scores (38 and 39 are represented in the same bin for data protection reasons). It does suggest, however, that a future revision of the scale should slightly increase item difficulty in order to decrease the ceiling effect. Alternatively, the ceiling effect may be seen as warranting a downward extension of the age span to start at, for example, 20 months in a future revision.

Table 31 and Figure 15 present descriptive statistics and histograms for the Productive Vocabulary subscale. As opposed to the Receptive Vocabulary subscale, the Productive Vocabulary subscale has the same items for all children aged 22–34 months, which is why the mean score increases from age group 22–23 months through age group 30–34 months. As shown in the table and histograms, the distribution goes from nonsignificantly right-skewed in age group 22–23 months to significantly left-skewed in the other two age groups, indicating that this subscale captures the development in these ages well.

Table 32 and Figure 16 present descriptive statistics and histograms for the Language Use subscale. This scale uses the same items for all children and

Table 30 Mean scores, standard deviations, range, and distributional characteristics for the subscale Receptive Vocabulary for the three age groups 22–23, 24–29, and 30–34 months. Age-dependent items. Values for the two split sample groups

Receptive Vocabulary	N	Missings	Mean	SD	Range	Skewness	Kurtosis
22–23 months	164	18	31.1	6.3	<21–37<	−1.26[1]	3.93[1]
Split sample	83/81		30.9/31.2	6.2/6.3	<21–37<	−1.24/−1.28	4.11/3.75
24–29 months	738	6	30.2	5.5	<18–39	−1.56[1]	7.00[1]
Split sample	370/368		30.3/30.0	5.1/6.0	<18–39	−1.31/−1.69	5.62/7.49
30–34 months	433	32	28.0	4.7	<18–37	−0.88[1]	4.54[1]
Split sample	218/215		28.0/27.9	4.6/4.7	<18–37	−0.85/−0.90	3.84/5.20

Note: For data protection, minimum and maximum scores are given using operators (<) if at least one score below or above the reported minimum/maximum is obtained by fewer than three individuals.
[1] Skewness/kurtosis test for normality significant, $p < 0.05$.

Table 31 Mean scores, standard deviations, range, and distributional characteristics for the subscale Productive Vocabulary for the three age groups 22–23, 24–29, and 30–34 months. Values for the two split sample groups

Productive Vocabulary	N	Missings	Mean	SD	Range	Skewness	Kurtosis
22–23 months	166	16	29.5	14.5	<10–59<	0.17	2.32[1]
Split sample	84/82		29.4/29.5	14.3/14.6	<10–59<	0.24/0.10	2.28/2.35
24–29 months	741	3	38.5	15.7	<5–68<	−0.31[1]	2.40[1]
Split sample	372/369		38.4/38.6	16.0/15.6	<5–68<	−0.28/−0.33	2.24/2.57
30–34 months	435	30	48.7	14.2	<15–70	−0.86[1]	3.15
Split sample	219/216		48.1/49.4	14.3/14.1	<15–70	−0.90/−0.82	3.19/3.06

Note: For data protection, minimum and maximum scores are given using operators (<) if at least one score below or above the reported minimum/maximum is obtained by fewer than three individuals.

[1] Skewness/kurtosis test for normality significant, $p < 0.05$.

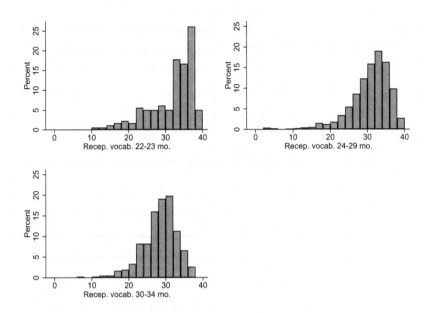

Figure 14 Distribution of scores on the Receptive Vocabulary subscale for the three age groups 22–23, 24–29, and 30–34 months. Age-dependent items

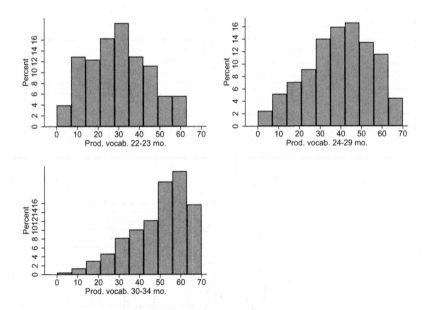

Figure 15 Distribution of scores on the Productive Vocabulary subscale for the three age groups 22–23, 24–29, and 30–34 months

Table 32 Mean scores, standard deviations, range, and distributional characteristics for the subscale Language Use for the three age groups 22–23, 24–29, and 30–34 months. Values for the two split sample groups

Language Use	N	Missings	Mean	SD	Range	Skewness	Kurtosis
22–23 months	166	16	4.3	2.5	0–10	0.31	2.60
Split sample	84/82		4.6/4.1	2.5/2.4	0–10	0.32/0.30	2.61/2.55
24–29 months	741	3	5.4	2.7	0–10	–0.07	2.22[1]
Split sample	372/369		5.4/5.4	2.7/2.6	0–10	–0.02/–0.13	2.16/2.31
30–34 months	435	30	6.9	2.6	0–10	–0.72[1]	2.83
Split sample	219/216		6.8/7.1	2.7/2.6	0–10	–0.67/–0.76	2.74/2.93

[1] Skewness/kurtosis test for normality significant, $p < 0.05$.

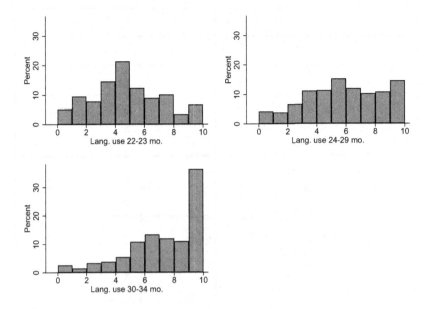

Figure 16 Distribution of scores on the decontextualized
Language Use subscale for the three age groups 22–23, 24–29,
and 30–34 months

accordingly shows an increase in mean score across the age groups and a more left-skewed distribution of scores with higher age groups. In the oldest children, there is a clear ceiling effect.

Table 33 and Figure 17 present descriptive statistics and histograms for the Communicative Skills subscale. The same items are used for all ages, and accordingly the mean score increases and the distribution becomes left-skewed with higher age groups.

4.8.2 Relation of Subscale Scores to Gender and Family Socioeconomic Status

The relation of gender and family SES to language development is well-documented, but less so in toddlers than in older children. However, gender and SES are clearly related to all four subscales of our language assessment instrument.

Table 34 shows that girls obtain significantly higher scores on average on all four subscales. The gender effect size is largest for Productive Vocabulary and Communicative Skills and smallest for Receptive Vocabulary. It is interesting that the gender effect is so different for the

Table 33 Mean scores, standard deviations, range, and distributional characteristics for the subscale Communicative Skills for the three age groups 22–23, 24–29, and 30–34 months. Values for the two split sample groups

Communicative Skills	N	Missings	Mean	SD	Range	Skewness	Kurtosis
22–23 months	166	16	35.0	11.0	<16–56<	0.10	2.75
Split sample	84/82		35.6/34.5	12.1/11.1	<16–56<	−0.03/0.25	2.77/2.76
24–29 months	741	3	41.8	13.2	<12–67<	−0.31[1]	2.51[1]
Split sample	372/369		42.0/41.7	13.0/13.8	<16–56<	−0.25/−0.34	2.40/2.58
30–34 months	435	30	49.0	12.9	<19–69	−0.70[1]	3.04
Split sample	219/216		48.9/49.2	13.0/13.0	<16–56<	−0.79/−0.60	3.27/22.78

Note: For data protection, minimum and maximum scores are given using operators (<) if at least one score below or above the reported minimum/maximum is obtained by fewer than three individuals.

[1] Skewness/kurtosis test for normality significant, $p < 0.05$.

Table 34 Mean scores (SDs) for 2-year-old boys and girls, effect size and significance of the gender difference on each subscale

Subscale	N	Boys	N	Girls	d	p
Receptive Vocabulary	710	29.1 (5.6)	633	30.1 (5.3)	0.18	0.001
Productive Vocabulary	734	38.0 (16.8)	642	42.9 (16.0)	0.30	0.001
Language Use	734	5.4 (2.8)	642	6.1 (2.8)	0.25	0.001
Communication	734	41.1 (14.2)	645	45.1 (13.5)	0.29	0.001

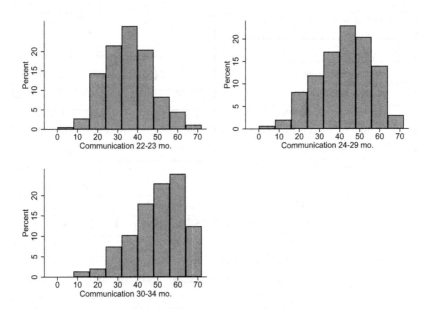

Figure 17 Distribution of scores on the Communicative Skills subscale for the three age groups 22–23, 24–29, and 30–34 months.

two vocabulary measures. However, the gender effect is somewhat smaller for the Receptive Vocabulary subscale than for all of the other three subscales. One possible interpretation is that boys trail girls to a lesser extent in receptive compared to productive language skills (Productive Vocabulary, Language Use, and Communication all being productive/expressive language skills). An alternative interpretation is that boys' perceived language skills tend to be underestimated by educators (and perhaps others as well). Recall that the Productive Vocabulary, Language Use, and Communication subscales are all completed by the educator based on the educator's estimation of the child's skills. However, for *LA 3–6*, the gender effect sizes for the Communication subscale (completed by the educator) were generally not of larger (or smaller) magnitude than the gender effect sizes for subscales that were direct tests. But clearly, the gender effects are large enough for all four subscales to warrant gender-specific norms.

Table 35 shows the correlations of each subscale with three SES variables: maternal education, paternal education, and household income. The correlations tended to be a little stronger with maternal and paternal education than with household income, but the confidence intervals indicate that the strengths of the correlations were generally not significant between the SES variables. Likewise, there was little difference in the strength between the correlations across the subscales.

Just as for *LA 3–6*, correlations between the subscale measures of *LA 3–6* and SES may serve as a tentative validation of the measures, because previous research has consistently found SES correlations with child language skills. However, a general finding in the literature is that associations between gender and child language outcomes become weaker through childhood (e.g., Wallentin, 2009), whereas SES associations with language and educational outcomes persist or even become stronger through the school ages (Sirin, 2005). Therefore, an assessment instrument should not take child SES into account or correct scores for SES just because a lower score is "expected" from a child with a low SES background. Differences in outcomes contingent on SES do not reflect temporary developmental differences like those contingent on gender do, but they may be associated with different learning opportunities in the home, which ECEC may help counter.

Table 35 Zero-order correlation (with 95% CIs) between parental SES variables and language outcomes. $N = 785–1,377$

Subscale	Maternal education	Paternal education	Household income
Receptive Vocabulary	0.20 (0.15–0.25)	0.16 (0.11–0.22)	0.10 (0.03–0.17)
Productive Vocabulary	0.09 (0.04–0.14)	0.15 (0.10–0.20)	0.09 (0.02–0.16)
Language Use	0.12 (0.07–0.17)	0.15 (0.09–0.20)	0.16 (0.09–0.23)
Communication	0.11 (0.06–0.16)	0.13 (0.08–0.18)	0.12 (0.05–0.19)
Summary score	0.15 (0.10–0.21)	0.18 (0.12–0.23)	0.15 (0.08–0.22)

Note: All correlations were significant at $p < 0.001$ except household income correlated with Receptive Vocabulary ($p = 0.006$) and Productive Vocabulary ($p = 0.013$).

4.9 Psychometric Qualities of the Instrument

4.9.1 Internal Consistency

Cronbach's alpha coefficients for the subscales for each age group were computed to evaluate internal consistency and are shown in Table 36. The alpha values were high, indicating high internal consistency. The lowest values were for the subscale Language Use, but note that this subscale consists of just five items. Recall also that the Productive Vocabulary and Language Use subscales were taken from an existing instrument; the alpha values obtained in the present norming sample were very similar to those originally reported for the instruments (Productive Vocabulary = 0.98, Language Use = 0.88; Bleses, Jensen, et al., 2018). The range of item-total correlations, indicating the correlation of each item with the overall scale, suggest that the scales have good consistency. A quite low item-total correlation of a single item in the Receptive Vocabulary test for 30–34-month-olds suggests that this item should be replaced in a future revision of the instrument.

4.9.2 Internal Validity

Zero-order correlations were calculated to estimate associations between pairs of subscales. The correlations of the Receptive Vocabulary subscale had age group partialled out because of the difference in items given across the three age groups. The correlations are shown in Table 37. It is perhaps surprising that the strongest correlation was not that between Receptive and Productive Vocabulary. The correlations were strongest between the subscales completed by the educator. This is likely to be due, at least in part, to shared assessor variance. In other words, a child who, in the educator's recollection, has a large vocabulary is also likely to be recollected as having advanced decontextualized language use and communication skills. In as far as this explanation is true, it goes to suggest the importance of testing (i.e., with active child participation) in addition to scales relying solely on the educator's estimation and recollection of child skills.

Another, not incompatible, explanation for stronger correlations between the educator-completed subscales than with the Receptive Vocabulary test is that children are likely to differ in test-taking ability independent of language skills. Some children may play along with the educator's agenda, the test, while other children may not. In as far as this explanation is true, it suggests the importance of assessments of the child that do *not* directly involve the child in a test.

As is the case for the results report for *LA 3–6*, a summary score is computed but mainly for administrative purposes, as noted in Section 4.6.1.

Table 36 Cronbach's alpha and item-total correlation range. For Receptive Vocabulary, values are given for each age group

Subscale	All ages N = 1,342		22–23 mo. N = 164		24–29 mo. N = 738		30–34 mo. N = 433	
	Alpha	Item-total	Alpha	Item-total	Alpha	Item-total	Alpha	Item-total
Rec. Vocabulary			0.91	0.40–0.63	0.91	0.31–0.62	0.85	0.15–0.56
Prod. Vocabulary	0.97	0.26–0.75						
Language Use	0.85	0.74–0.82						
Communication	0.95	0.42–0.84						

Table 37 Zero-order correlations (with 95% CIs) between subscales, with the exception of correlations with Receptive Vocabulary, for which age group was partialled out. $N = 1,330–1,337$

Subscale	1	2	3
1. Receptive Vocabulary	-		
2. Productive Vocabulary	0.43 (0.39–0.47)	-	
3. Language Use	0.42 (0.37–0.46)	0.70 (0.67–0.73)	-
4. Communication	0.46 (0.42–0.50)	0.76 (0.73–0.79)	0.75 (0.72–0.77)

Note: All correlations were significant at $p < 0.001$.

4.9.3 External Validity

To externally validate the four subscales, a subsample of fifty-one children were tested using the Danish adaptation of the Receptive One-Word Picture Vocabulary Test (Martin & Brownell, 2011). Correlations of each subscale with raw scores on the Receptive One-Word Picture Vocabulary Test are shown in Table 38. The correlations with the external validation instrument were slightly stronger for the two vocabulary measures than for Language Use and Communication and generally similar to the strongest external validity correlations found for *LA 3–6* (Section 3.7.3). This indicates that assessment of 2-year-olds with *LA 2* is feasible and no less valid than assessment of older children with *LA 3–6*.

4.9.4 Test-Retest Reliability

Test-retest data are not available for children in the norming study. However, as noted, the subscales Productive Vocabulary and Language Use are from an existing instrument, the *CDI: Educator*. These two measures were previously evaluated for test-retest reliability by Bleses, Jensen, et al. (2018); the measures had been used as pretests and posttests in an early language and math intervention study (Bleses, Jensen, et al., 2020). The measurements were taken approximately seven months apart, which means that – just as for the test-retest evaluation of *LA 3–6* – the autocorrelation estimates are conservative because it cannot be assumed that all children's language skills develop at the same rate over such a relatively long period of time. For Productive Vocabulary, the test-retest correlation was $r = 0.68$. For Language Use, the correlation was $r = 0.54$.

These indirect measures of reliability suggest moderate autocorrelations. While it was not possible to provide measures of test-retest reliability for the

Table 38 Zero-order correlations (with 95% CIs) of each subscale with the Receptive One-Word Picture Vocabulary Test (raw scores). For the Receptive Vocabulary subscale, age group was partialled out. $N = 51$

Subscale	One-Word	*p*
Receptive Vocabulary	0.57 (0.35–0.73)	0.001
Productive Vocabulary	0.55 (0.32–0.72)	0.001
Language Use	0.49 (0.25–0.67)	0.001
Communication	0.44 (0.19–0.64)	0.001

Receptive Vocabulary subscale and the Communication Subscale, we expect to be able to do so in the future through collaboration on data analysis with municipalities and providers of IT platforms for the instrument.

4.9.5 Procedure for Establishing Percentile Scores

Just as for *LA 3–6*, we established percentile norms based on our norming sample. Because scores are strongly related to both age and gender, as evidenced in Sections 4.8.1 and 4.8.2, we developed age- and gender-specific norms. The percentile score corresponding to a raw score value x of a child at age a (in months) is based on considering all children of the same gender and with an age of +/− two months and tested with the same material. For *LA 2*, we used a simpler procedure than the regression procedure used for *LA 3–6* (see Section 3.7.4) to determine the score required to be on a given percentile. For *LA 2*, we smoothed the developmental curve by using the simple mean score for children of that gender at the given age, the two months preceding that age, and the two months following (that is, a five-month moving window). The procedure means that we "borrow data strength" from ages just above and below the age in question in a slightly different way than for *LA 3–6*. The change of approach was because the regression models did not converge. We are not sure why this is the case; one possibility is that it has to do with the lower *N* per month in *LA 2*. However, the purpose was, again, to iron out natural fluctuations causing anomalies in the normative development.

5 International Lessons to Be Learned from the Danish Assessment Program and Instrument Development

Early developmental delays, including those in the domain of language and literacy, are major risk factors for children's later educational attainment, and consequently, high-income countries like Denmark have increasingly implemented universal programs to screen children for developmental delay in the early years (Cairney et al., 2021). Such programs, including those targeting language, are typically situated in primary care facilities and implemented as part of general health surveillance programs. In Denmark, on the contrary, the national language assessment program is implemented and integrated with the universal ECEC program in Denmark.

Both the goals and the resources available for early screening will vary from country to country and must be considered in developing assessment programs. In addition, one must consider the resources available for following up children who seem to need intervention. If the child cannot receive intervention in an ECEC center or otherwise, the screening result may be of little use.

In this section we will describe some lessons learned from the national Danish educational language assessment program described in this Element, which may be useful for investigators developing similar measures in other languages. Early identification of children with language delay is, of course, a key element of all assessment programs, but the most important argument for placing the national language assessment program in the ECEC setting is the possibility of using the results of the language assessment to target children's individual needs in the ECEC setting. Educators can use the language screenings to obtain a detailed picture of the language development of each child and on that basis provide children with the opportunities for the learning they need. However, the potential of educational assessment programs is contingent on the ability of educators both to administer the assessments in a valid way and to use the results of the assessment to tailor the instruction to the needs of the children, both individually and in the group as a whole. Along with these principled reasons for turning to educators for early screening is a practical one: In many countries there is a shortage of speech and language professionals, and screening often has lower priority than service delivery.

Although issues of practicality for educator administration are important for the selection of scales and specific norms, it is also essential to utilize as much developmental information on the target language as possible, as was discussed and exemplified in Section 4.2. Which items show developmental change in the age range of interest and also show predictions of future development? Simple translation is unlikely to be a productive method for the development of these measures except in cases of highly similar languages and cultures.

One of the first lessons learned reflects our preliminary evidence that educators with little or no training in linguistics or test administration can deliver valid information on children's language development if the materials and instructions are sufficiently clear (see also Haghish et al., 2021). A tablet-based IT system for the administration of the language assessment provides the necessary support for the educators to administer the assessment instrument in a consistent and valid way. It also facilitates more complete and accurate data entry of children's responses. This technical support is essential, given the multiple demands on educator time and energy, and not least, it takes care of tallying scores and calculating norm-based assessment results. But training is also essential. Currently, it is the municipalities' own responsibility to introduce educators to the use of the instrument; anecdotal evidence suggests that this is done in very different ways, ranging from no introduction other than supplying the manual and materials to course work introduction with supportive facilities at the municipality level. It is likely that the administration and therefore also the validity of the instrument would benefit from a more systematic nationally aligned introduction to the administration of the language assessment (for example, workshops and certification procedures). While educators can administer language assessments that produce valid and reliable results, it is difficult to rely on parent report as part of the assessment instrument, because many parents, and disproportionately those at risk, fail to complete and submit the parent reports; in the case of immigrant families, language may also be a bottleneck in this regard. This is likely to be an issue in any country or context, therefore educator reports are preferable.

An overall consideration when asking ECEC educators to administer language tests is to recognize that the purpose differs from the usual purpose when educators interact with children. Usually, the task of the educator is to help children learn, succeed, and overcome obstacles. In a test situation, the purpose is quite different. The purpose is to get an accurate measurement of the child's skills and thus to succeed when the child has the ability to answer a test question correctly but to fail when they do not. Seeing children fail and recording that failure runs counter to the purpose of educators' normal professional interaction with children. This is a lesson we have learned during years of experience of training and observing ECEC educators administering assessments. Therefore, it is emphasized explicitly in our manuals that the purpose of the assessment is not to help the child score as high as possible but to ensure that the child's language skills are assessed as accurately as possible. At times in our communication with educators, we have compared helping the child too much to a situation when a pediatrician asks a potentially malnourished child to stand on their tiptoes to receive a sufficient height measurement to fit within developmental norms or helps a child with poor vision to pass a vision test by giving helpful hints. In such cases, children may miss out on adequate or correct intervention and support, which is obviously not in their best interests.

On a similar note, educators are used to giving children challenges that they can manage, perhaps with some help or scaffolding. Therefore, many educators find it troublesome or even unfair to the child to give them challenges that they are unlikely to be able to manage. This is the case for very hard items such as the word "parachute" for a 2½-year-old child, which few will know. However, to obtain a normal distribution of scores, or at least a distribution with some degree of differentiation between children at the high end of the scale, such very difficult items are, of course, necessary. The approach of ensuring that almost everybody "fails" at least on some items rather than ensuring that almost everybody succeeds on all items is strange to educators as well as to parents. However, this approach is necessary for this type of norm-referenced rather than criterion-based approach to language assessment in order that all children receive an assessment of their language skills that is optimally accurate and maximizes its value in informing and providing the best intervention.

Ultimately, universal language assessment – like any kind of diagnostic work – is only worthwhile if there are effective and practical interventions to follow. This is a highly challenging requirement. In the present project, a valuable feature was the fact that the majority of Danish municipalities use nationally endorsed language assessment material. In a recent survey of ECEC directors in the municipalities, to which 91 of 98 directors responded, more than 80 replied that they used the current material (Socialministeriets Benchmarking Enhed, 2020). The use of the same instrument across the vast majority of ECEC centers enables a broad discussion of sophisticated ways, both at local and national level, to monitor children's early language development and to use the data for the continuous development of the ECEC area. Fostering communication between those who conduct assessments and those who design and provide intervention is absolutely essential but not nearly as widespread as it needs to be. At the same time, the report indicates that the municipalities take quite varied approaches in terms of how much they embed the language assessment in the ECEC setting.

Much less is known about how educators actually use the results of the language assessments to target the needs of individual children and how to facilitate that process. The above-mentioned report suggests that there is a large potential in supporting the municipalities and centers in translating the results of the assessment to educational practices that match the needs of the children. Only a little more than half of the municipalities support ECEC centers in actively using the results of the language assessments to guide the stimulation of children's language development, and even fewer municipalities support the collaboration with parents on their child's language development on the basis of assessment results (Socialministeriets Benchmarking Enhed, 2020). But although it is normally desirable to see a strong link between language assessment procedures and follow-up procedures to help language development in children who seem to need it, there is also a possible danger that needs to be considered. If municipalities, ECEC leaders, or individual educators have too much of an incentive to avoid low scores on language assessments, there is a risk that educators, who know the assessment instruments well, will tailor their daily language activities and language stimulation to the tasks that the child needs to perform during assessment. Although these skills are certainly important, direct "teaching to the test" is unlikely to produce lasting benefits for the child and may ultimately result in the overestimation of language skills, with ensuing under-identification of children who need real language stimulation. This is a point that we have stressed repeatedly when offering courses or talks about our materials, but we have little knowledge about the extent of the problem.

There is a need for researcher–educator collaboration in realizing the potential of language assessments. Recent RCT (randomized control trial) studies of low-cost language and school readiness enhancement programs for ECEC settings targeting children aged 1–5 years have shown substantial effects on language domains targeted in the language assessments (Bleses, Højen, Dale, et al., 2018; Bleses, Højen, Justice, et al., 2018; Bleses, Jensen, Høyen, et al., 2021; Bleses, Jensen, et al., 2020). All these studies also suggest that even though interventions on average are implemented as intended, there is substantial variation across classrooms and centers, suggesting that more direct implementation support of educators and leaders is necessary for all children to benefit from interventions (Bleses, Jensen, Høyen, et al., 2021).

Appropriate interventions are becoming more available; the goal must be to use them more effectively. A closer linkage between assessment instruments and interventions may be a fruitful way to move forward. Response-to-intervention (RTI) models, briefly discussed earlier, suggest a useful framework here. In RTI, children are not permanently assigned to "typically developing" or "special needs" groups. In each phase of instruction, children experiencing difficulty are given increasing levels of support – for example, small groups or one-to-one intervention – based on their performance. As their performance improves, the services are reduced.

We conclude with a more general reflection from this project on early language assessment. Language assessment administered to children by educators in an ECEC context is a way of raising educators' awareness of language development in children in general as well as supporting the development of language skills in individual children. The experience in Denmark has been one of initial skepticism among some, but not all, portions of the ECEC community, but there has been an increasing awareness of the potentials of language assessment over the years. Skepticism of early assessment in general has become virtually nonexistent in the ECEC landscape by now, about fifteen years after the introduction of the first instrument, although opinions vary on how, when, and who to assess.

We think an important role in this "cultural change" has been our efforts to obtain feedback from ECEC and speech-language practitioners in developing and revising our instruments. Inviting future users to take part in the development of assessment also serves to increase face validity when launching the instruments. User suggestions may increase the validity of the measure or they may be worthwhile just because they increase the likelihood of adoption and careful administration, which may otherwise be highly variable given the multiple demands on ECEC educators.

The materials and manuals for both language assessment instruments may be shared upon request to the Danish Ministry for Children and Education. The first author can assist in this regard, and the authors in general are positive towards assisting in adapting the instruments.

Appendix: List of Studies Included in Meta-Analysis of Early Predictors of Later Outcomes

Aro, T., Eklund, K., Nurmi, J.-E., & Poikkeus, A.-M. (2012). Early language and behavioral regulation skills as predictors of social outcomes. *Journal of Speech, Language, and Hearing Research*, *55*(2), 395–408. https://doi.org/10.1044/1092-4388(2011/10-0245)

Bartl-Pokorny, K. D., Marschik, P. B., Sachse, S., Green, V. A., Zhang, D., Van Der Meer, L., et al. (2013). Tracking development from early speech-language acquisition to reading skills at age 13. *Developmental Neurorehabilitation*, *16*(3), 188–195. https://doi.org/10.3109/17518423.2013.773101

Blair, C., Ursache, A., Greenberg, M., & Vernon-Feagans, L. (2015). Multiple aspects of self-regulation uniquely predict mathematics but not letter–word knowledge in the early elementary grades. *Developmental Psychology*, *51*(4), 459.

Bleses, D., Makransky, G., Dale, P. S., Højen, A., & Ari, B. A. (2016). Early productive vocabulary predicts academic achievement 10 years later. *Applied Psycholinguistics*, *37*(6), 1461–1476. https://doi.org/10.1017/S0142716416000060

Blums, A., Belsky, J., Grimm, K., & Chen, Z. (2017). Building links between early socioeconomic status, cognitive ability, and math and science achievement. *Journal of Cognition and Development*, *18*(1), 16–40.

Justice, L. M., Bowles, R. P., Pence Turnbull, K. L., & Skibbe, L. E. (2009). School readiness among children with varying histories of language difficulties. *Developmental Psychology*, *45*(2), 460.

Lee, J. (2011). Size matters: Early vocabulary as a predictor of language and literacy competence. *Applied Psycholinguistics*, *32*(01), 69–92.

Lyytinen, P., Eklund, K., & Lyytinen, H. (2005). Language development and literacy skills in late-talking toddlers with and without familial risk for dyslexia. *Annals of Dyslexia*, *55*(2), 166–192.

Pentimonti, J. M., Murphy, K. A., Justice, L. M., Logan, J. A. R., & Kaderavek, J. N. (2016). School readiness of children with language impairment: Predicting literacy skills from pre-literacy and social–behavioural dimensions. *International Journal of Language and Communication Disorders*, *51*(2), 148–161. https://doi.org/10.1111/1460-6984.12193

Poll, G. H., & Miller, C. A. (2013). Late talking, typical talking, and weak language skills at middle childhood. *Learning and Individual Differences*, *26*, 177–184.

Rescorla, L. (2005). Age 13 language and reading outcomes in late-talking toddlers. *Journal of Speech, Language, and Hearing Research*, *48*(2), 459–472. https://doi.org/10.1044/1092-4388(2005/031)

Tamis-LeMonda, C. S., Song, L., Luo, R., Kuchirko, Y., Kahana-Kalman, R., Yoshikawa, H., & Raufman, J. (2014). Children's vocabulary growth in English and Spanish across early development and associations with school readiness skills. *Developmental Neuropsychology*, *39*(2), 69–87. https://doi.org/10.1080/87565641.2013.827198

References

Bentler, P. M., & Bonett, D. G. (1980). Significance tests and goodness of fit in the analysis of covariance structures. *Psychological Bulletin, 88*(3), 588–606. https://doi.org/10.1037/0033-2909.88.3.588

Bleses, D., Basbøll, H., & Vach, W. (2011). Is Danish difficult to acquire? Evidence from Nordic past-tense studies. *Language and Cognitive Processes, 26*(8), 1193–1231.

Bleses, D., Hvidman, C., Munkedal, S., et al. (2018). *Elever med svage kompetencer i sprog og læseforståelse. Forskningskortlægning af effektive indsatser, risikofaktorer og sammenhænge med anden læring* [*Students with low language and reading comprehension skills: A systematic review of interventions, risk factors and relation to skill development*]. Styrelsen for Undervisning og Kvalitet [Agency for Teaching and Quality].

Bleses, D., Højen, A., Dale, P. S., et al. (2018). Effective language and literacy instruction: Evaluating the importance of scripting and group size components. *Early Childhood Research Quarterly, 42*, 256–269. https://doi .org/10.1016/j.ecresq.2017.10.002

Bleses, D., Højen, A., Justice, L. M., et al. (2018). The effectiveness of a large-scale language and preliteracy intervention: The SPELL randomized-controlled-trial in Denmark. *Child Development, 89*(4), e342–e363. https://doi.org/10.1111/cdev .12859

Bleses, D., Jensen, P., Højen, A., et al. (2018). An educator-administered measure of language development in young children. *Infant Behavior and Development, 52*, 104–113. https://doi.org/10.1016/j.infbeh.2018.06.002

Bleses, D., Jensen, P., Højen, A., et al. (2021). Implementing toddler interventions at scale: The case of "We learn together." *Early Childhood Research Quarterly, 57*, 12–26. https://doi.org/10.1016/j.ecresq.2021.04.008

Bleses, D., Jensen, P., Slot, P., et al. (2020). Low-cost teacher-implemented intervention improves toddlers' language and math skills. *Early Childhood Research Quarterly, 53*, 64–76. https://doi.org/10.1016/j.ecresq.2020.03.001

Bleses, D., Lum, J. A. G., Højen, A., et al. (2011). Sprogvurderingsmateriale til 3-årige, Inden skolestart og i Børnehaveklassen. Metodisk oversigt [Language Assessment Instrument for 3-year-olds before school start and in kindergarten]. *Working Papers in Language Acquisition – University of Southern Denmark, 13.* https://static.sdu.dk/Flexpaper/aspnet/pdf/E-print_ 13_2011.pdf

Bleses, D., Makransky, G., Dale, P. S., et al. (2016). Early productive vocabulary predicts academic achievement 10 years later. *Applied Psycholinguistics*, *37*(6), 1461–1476. https://doi.org/10.1017/S0142716416000060

Bleses, D., Vach, W., Jørgensen, R. N., et al. (2010). The internal validity and acceptability of the Danish SI-3: A language-screening instrument for 3-year-olds. *Journal of Speech, Language, and Hearing Research*, *53*(2), 490–507.

Bleses, D., Vach, W., Slott, M., et al. (2008a). The Danish communicative developmental inventories: Validity and main developmental trends. *Journal of Child Language*, *35*(3), 651–669. https://doi.org/10.1017/s030500 0907008574

Bleses, D., Vach, W., Slott, M., et al. (2008b). Early vocabulary development in Danish and other languages: A CDI-based comparison. *Journal of Child Language*, *35*(3), 619–650. https://doi.org/10.1017/S0305000908008714

Bleses, D., Vach, W., Wehberg, S., et al. (2007). *Tidlig kommunikativ udvikling: Et værktøj til beskrivelse af sprogtilegnelse* [*Early communicative development: A tool for the description of language acquisition*]. Syddansk Universitetsforlag [University Press of Southern Denmark].

Bornstein, M. H., Hahn, C.-S., & Haynes, O. M. (2004). Specific and general language performance across early childhood: Stability and gender considerations. *First Language*, *24*(3), 267–304. https://doi.org/10.1177/014272 3704045681

Bornstein, M. H., & Hendricks, C. (2012). Basic language comprehension and production in >100,000 young children from sixteen developing nations. *Journal of Child Language*, *39*(4), 899–918. https://doi.org/10.1017/S03050 00911000407

Bosch, L., & Sebastián-Gallés, N. (2003). Simultaneous bilingualism and the perception of a language-specific vowel contrast in the first year of life. *Language and Speech*, *46*, 217–243.

Cairney, D. G., Kazmi, A., Delahunty, L., et al. (2021). The predictive value of universal preschool developmental assessment in identifying children with later educational difficulties: A systematic review. *PloS One*, *16*(3), e0247299. https://doi.org/10.1371/journal.pone.0247299

Catts, H. W., Herrera, S., Nielsen, D. C., et al. (2015). Early prediction of reading comprehension within the simple view framework. *Reading and Writing*, *28*(9), 1407–1425. https://doi.org/10.1007/s11145-015-9576-x

Clausen, M. C., & Fox-Boyer, A. (2017). Phonological development of Danish-speaking children: A normative cross-sectional study. *Clinical Linguistics & Phonetics*, *31*(6), 440–458. https://doi.org/10.1080/02699206 .2017.1308014

Crystal, D. (2010). *The Cambridge encyclopedia of language*. Cambridge University Press.

Dale, P. S. (1996). Parent report assessment of language and communication. In K. N. Cole, P. S. Dale, & D. J. Thal (eds.), *Assessment of communication and language* (pp. 161–182). Brookes.

Dale, P. S., Harlaar, N., & Plomin, R. (2005). Telephone testing and teacher assessment of reading skills in 7-year-olds: I. Substantial correspondence for a sample of 5544 children and for extremes. *Reading and Writing, 18*(5), 385–400. https://doi.org/10.1007/s11145-004-8130-z

Danish Ministry for Social Affairs. (2015). Statistik om dagtilbudsområdet [Numbers and statistics about daycare].

Dollaghan, C. (2013). Late talker as a clinical category: A critical evaluation. In L. Rescorla & P. S. Dale (eds.), *Late talkers: Language development, interventions, and outcomes* (pp. 5–21). Brookes.

Dunn, L. M., & Dunn, D. M. (2007). *Peabody Picture Vocabulary Test (PPVT-4)*. Pearson Assessments.

Fenson, L., Marchman, V. A., Thal, D., et al. (2007). *MacArthur-Bates Communicative Development Inventories: User's guide and technical manual* (2nd ed.). Brookes.

Fernald, A., Marchman, V. A., & Weisleder, A. (2013). SES differences in language processing skill and vocabulary are evident at 18 months. *Developmental Science, 16*(2), 234–248. https://doi.org/10.1111/desc.12019

Friend, M., & Keplinger, M. (2008). Reliability and validity of the Computerized Comprehension Task (CCT): Data from American English and Mexican Spanish infants. *Journal of Child Language, 35*(1), 77–98.

Friend, M., Schmitt, S. A., & Simpson, A. M. (2012). Evaluating the predictive validity of the Computerized Comprehension Task: Comprehension predicts production. *Developmental Psychology, 48*(1), 136.

Fuchs, D., Fuchs, L. S., & Compton, D. L. (2012). Smart RTI: A next-generation approach to multilevel prevention. *Exceptional Children, 78*(3), 263–279. https://doi.org/10.1177/001440291207800301

Garmann, N. G., Romøren, A. S. H., Flygstad, N., et al. (2019). Språkkartlegging i norske barnehager: En pilotundersøkelse av foreldres og barnehageansattes rapportering av norsktalende tre-åringers språkferdigheter ved hjelp av CDI III. [Language assessment in Norwegian childcare centers: A pilot investigation of parental and educator report of native Norwegian three-year-olds' language skills using CDI III]. *Rask, 49*, 87–102. www.sdu.dk/-/media/files/om_sdu/institutter/isk/forskningspublikationer/rask/rask+49/rask+49_87–103.pdf

Gibson, T. A., Oller, D. K., Jarmulowicz, L., et al. (2012). The receptive–expressive gap in the vocabulary of young second-language learners: Robustness and possible mechanisms. *Bilingualism: Language and Cognition, 15*(1), 102–116. https://doi.org/10.1017/S13667289100 00490

Gross, M., Buac, M., & Kaushanskaya, M. (2014). Conceptual scoring of receptive and expressive vocabulary measures in simultaneous and sequential bilingual children. *American Journal of Speech-Language Pathology, 23* (4), 574–586. https://doi.org/10.1044/2014_AJSLP-13-0026

Haghish, E. F., Vach, W., Bleses, D., et al. (2021). Estimating measurement error in child language assessments administered by daycare educators in large scale intervention studies. *PloS One, 16*(11), e0255414. https://doi.org /10.1371/journal.pone.0255414

Hammer, C. S., Hoff, E., Uchikoshi, Y., et al. (2014). The language and literacy development of young dual language learners: A critical review. *Early Childhood Research Quarterly, 29*(4), 715–733. https://doi.org/10.1016/j .ecresq.2014.05.008

Hansen, P. (2017). What makes a word easy to acquire? The effects of word class, frequency, imageability and phonological neighbourhood density on lexical development. *First Language, 37*(2), 205–225. https://doi.org/10 .1177/0142723716679956

Harlaar, N., Hayiou-Thomas, M. E., Dale, P. S., et al. (2008). Why do preschool language abilities correlate with later reading? A twin study. *Journal of Speech, Language, and Hearing Research, 51*(3), 688–705. https://doi.org/10 .1044/1092-4388(2008/049)

Hart, B., & Risley, T. R. (1995). *Meaningful differences in the everyday experience of young American children*. Brookes.

Hemsley, G., Holm, A., & Dodd, B. (2010). Patterns in diversity: Lexical learning in Samoan-English bilingual children. *International Journal of Speech-Language Pathology, 12*(4), 362–374. https://doi.org/10.3109/ 17549501003721064

Hendrickson, K., Mitsven, S., Poulin-Dubois, D., et al. (2015). Looking and touching: What extant approaches reveal about the structure of early word knowledge. *Developmental Science, 18*(5), 723–735. https://doi.org/10.1111/ desc.12250

Hendrickson, K., Poulin-Dubois, D., Zesiger, P., et al. (2017). Assessing a continuum of lexical–semantic knowledge in the second year of life: A multimodal approach. *Journal of Experimental Child Psychology, 158*, 95–111. https://doi.org/10.1016/j.jecp.2017.01.003

Hoff, E. (2006). How social contexts support and shape language development. *Developmental Review*, *26*(1), 55–88. https://doi.org/10.1016/j.dr.2005.11.002

Hoff, E. (2013). Interpreting the early language trajectories of children from low-SES and language minority homes: Implications for closing achievement gaps. *Developmental Psychology*, *49*(1), 4.

Hoff, E. (2014). *Language Development* (5th ed.). Wadsworth.

Hoff, E. (2015). Language development in bilingual children. In E. L. Bavin & L. R. Naigles (eds.), *The Cambridge Handbook of Child Language* (2nd ed., pp. 481–503). Cambridge University Press.

Hoff, E., Core, C., & Bridges, K. A. (2008). Non-word repetition assesses phonological memory and is related to vocabulary development in 20- to 24-month-olds. *Journal of Child Language*, *35*, 903–916.

Hoff, E., Core, C., Place, S., et al. (2012). Dual language exposure and early bilingual development. *Journal of Child Language*, *39*(1), 1–27. https://doi.org/10.1017/S0305000910000759

Huttenlocher, J., Waterfall, H., Vasilyeva, M., et al. (2010). Sources of variability in children's language growth. *Cognitive Psychology*, *61*(4), 343–365.

Højen, A., Bleses, D., Jensen, P., et al. (2019). Patterns of educational achievement among groups of immigrant children in Denmark emerge already in preschool second-language and preliteracy skills. *Applied Psycholinguistics*, *40*(4), 853–875. https://doi.org/10.1017/S0142716418000814

Højen, A., Hoff, E., Bleses, D., et al. (2021). The relation of home literacy environments to language and preliteracy skills in single- and dual-language children in Danish childcare. *Early Childhood Research Quarterly*, *55*, 312–325. https://doi.org/10.1016/j.ecresq.2020.12.007

Kamhi, A. G., & Catts, H. W. (2012). *Language and reading disabilities* (3rd ed.). Pearson.

Klem, M., Gustafsson, J.-E., & Hagtvet, B. (2015). The dimensionality of language ability in four-year-olds: Construct validation of a language screening tool. *Scandinavian Journal of Educational Research*, *59*(2), 195–213.

Landersø, R., & Heckman, J. J. (2017). The Scandinavian fantasy: The sources of intergenerational mobility in Denmark and the US. *The Scandinavian Journal of Economics*, *119*(1), 178–230.

Lee, J. (2011). Size matters: Early vocabulary as a predictor of language and literacy competence. *Applied Psycholinguistics*, *32*(01), 69–92.

Leonard, L. B. (2014). *Children with Specific Language Impairment* (2nd ed.). MIT Press.

Lightfoot, C., Cole, M., & Cole, S. R. (2013). *The development of children* (7th ed.). Worth.

Luria, A. R. (1981). *Language and cognition*. Wiley.

Marchman, V. A., & Dale, P. S. (2018). Assessing receptive and expressive vocabulary in child language. In A. M. B. de Groot & P. Hagoort (eds.), *Research methods in psycholinguistics and the neurobiology of language: A practical guide* (pp. 40–67). Wiley.

Martin, N. A., & Brownell, R. (2011). *Receptive One-Word Picture Vocabulary Test 4*. Academic Therapy Publications.

McLeod, S., Crowe, K., & Shahaeian, A. (2015). Intelligibility in context scale: Normative and validation data for English-speaking preschoolers. *Language, Speech, and Hearing Services in Schools*, *46*(3), 266–276. https://doi.org/10.1044/2015_LSHSS-14-0120

National Early Literacy Panel. (2008). *Developing early literacy*. National Institute for Literacy.

Nelson, H. D., Nygren, P., Walker, M., & Panoscha, R. (2006). Screening for speech and language delay in preschool children: Systematic evidence review for the US Preventive Services Task Force. *Pediatrics*, *117*(2), e298–e319.

Nielsen, H., Jensen, P., Bleses, D., et al. (2017). *Forskningsbaseret evaluering af Fremtidens Dagtilbud: Undersøgelse af indsatsens implementering og effekter* [*Research-based evaluation of daycare of the future: Examination of implementation and effects of the intervention*]. https://dk.ramboll.com/-/media/files/rm/rapporter/forskningsbaseret-evalueringsrapport-fremtidens-dagtilbud.pdf?la=da

O'Neill, D. K. (2007). The Language Use Inventory for young children: A parent-report measure of pragmatic language development for 18- to 47-month-old children. *Journal of Speech, Language, and Hearing Research*, *50*(1), 214–228. https://doi.org/10.1044/1092-4388(2007/017)

Paradis, J., Genesee, F., & Crago, M. B. (2021). *Dual language development and disorders* (3rd ed.). Brookes.

Paul, R., Norbury, C., & Gosse, C. (2018). *Language disorders from infancy through adolescence* (5th ed.). Elsevier.

Pearson. (2007). *PPVT 4 – EVT 2. Technical information*. https://support.pearson.com/usclinical/servlet/fileField?entityId=ka00N000000sibPQAQ&field=Attachments__Body__s

Poll, G. H., & Miller, C. A. (2013). Late talking, typical talking, and weak language skills at middle childhood. *Learning and Individual Differences*, *26*, 177–184.

Raudenbush, S. W., & Bryk, A. S. (2002). *Hierarchical linear models: Applications and data analysis methods* (Vol. 1). Sage.

Rescorla, L. (2005). Age 13 language and reading outcomes in late-talking toddlers. *Journal of Speech, Language, and Hearing Research, 48*(2), 459–472. https://doi.org/10.1044/1092-4388(2005/031)

Rescorla, L., & Dale, P. S. (eds.). (2013). *Late talkers: Language development, interventions, and outcomes*. Brookes.

Restrepo, M. A. (1998). Identifiers of predominantly Spanish-speaking children with language impairment. *Journal of Speech, Language, and Hearing Research, 41*(6), 1398–1411.

Reusch, S. (2006). *Kortlægning af PPRs opgaver over for børn i 0-6-års alderen i perioden 1/1 – 31/12 2005* [*Mapping of the tasks of speech pathologists for children aged 0–6 from January 1 to December 31, 2005*]. UNI-C.

Ribot, K. M., & Hoff, E. (2014). "¿Cómo estas?" "I'm good." Conversational code-switching is related to profiles of expressive and receptive proficiency in Spanish-English bilingual toddlers. *International Journal of Behavioral Development, 38*(4), 333–341. https://doi.org/10.1177/0165025414533225

Roberts, J. E., Burchinal, M., & Durham, M. (1999). Parents' report of vocabulary and grammatical development of African American preschoolers: Child and environmental associations. *Child Development, 70*(1), 92–106. https://doi.org/10.1111/1467-8624.00008

Sattler, J. (2001). *Assessment of children: Cognitive applications* (4th ed.). Sattler.

Saxton, M. (2017). *Child language: Acquisition and development* (2nd ed.). Sage.

Sirin, S. R. (2005). Socioeconomic status and academic achievement: A meta-analytic review of research. *Review of Educational Research, 75*(3), 417–453. https://doi.org/10.3102/00346543075003417

Snow, C. E., & van Hemel, S. B. (2008). *Early childhood assessment: Why, what, and how*. National Academies Press. https://doi.org/10.17226/12446

Socialministeriets Benchmarking Enhed. (2020). Analyse af kommunernes arbejde med sprogudvikling på dagtilbudsområdet [Analysis of municipalities' efforts in language development in childcare]. https://benchmark.dk/media/17851/kortlaegning_af_kommunernes_arbejde_med_sprogud vikling_paa_dagtilbudsomraadet_tilg.pdf

Wallentin, M. (2009). Putative sex differences in verbal abilities and language cortex: A critical review. *Brain and Language, 108*(3), 175–183. https://doi.org/10.1016/j.bandl.2008.07.001

Wehberg, S., Vach, W., Bleses, D., et al. (2007). Danish children's first words: Analysing longitudinal data based on monthly CDI parental reports. *First Language, 27*(4), 361–383. https://doi.org/10.1177/0142723707081723

Wells, G. (2007). The mediating role of discoursing in activity. *Mind, Culture, and Activity, 14*(3), 160–177. https://doi.org/10.1080/10749030701316300

Williams, K. T. (2007). *EVT-2: Expressive Vocabulary Test*. Pearson Assessments.

World Economic Forum. (2020). *The global social mobility report 2020: Equality, opportunity and a new economic imperative*. World Economic Forum.

Acknowledgments

The present as well as previous versions of the language assessment instruments were funded by Danish ministries. We thank several people who have been involved in the development of past and present versions of the instruments, including Werner Vach, Jarred Lum, Guido Makransky, Margaret Friend, Rune N. Jørgensen, Søren Munkedal, Lau M. Andersen, and Torben Worm.

Cambridge Elements ⚌

Research Methods for Developmental Science

Brett Laursen
Florida Atlantic University

Brett Laursen is a professor of psychology at Florida Atlantic University. He is editor-in-chief of the *International Journal of Behavioral Development*, where he previously served as the founding editor of the Methods and Measures section. Professor Laursen received his Ph.D. in child psychology from the Institute of Child Development at the University of Minnesota and an honorary doctorate from Örebro University, Sweden. He is a docent professor of educational psychology at the University of Helsinki and a Fellow of the American Psychological Association (Division 7, Developmental), the Association for Psychological Science, and the International Society for the Study of Behavioural Development. Professor Laursen is the coeditor of the *Handbook of Developmental Research Methods* and the *Handbook of Peer Interactions, Relationships, and Groups*.

About the Series

Each offering in this series will focus on methodological innovations and contemporary strategies to assess adjustment and measure change, empowering scholars of developmental science who seek to optimally match their research questions to pioneering methods and quantitative analyses.

Cambridge Elements $\equiv$

Research Methods for Developmental Science

Printed in the United States
by Baker & Taylor Publisher Services